How to Study the Bible

How to Study the Bible

by
John MacArthur, Jr.

MOODY PRESS
CHICAGO

© 1982 by
JOHN F. MACARTHUR, JR.

Moody Press Edition, 1985
Original title: *Lighting the Path*

All Scripture quotations, unless otherwise noted, are from the *New Scofield Reference Bible, King James Version,* © 1967 by Oxford University Press, Inc. Reprinted by permission.

ISBN: 0-8024-5105-5

3 4 5 6 7 Printing/EP/Year 91 90 89 88 87 86

Printed in the United States of America

Contents

These Bible studies are taken from messages delivered by Pastor-Teacher John MacArthur, Jr., at Grace Community Church in Panorama City, California. The recorded messages themselves may be purchased as a series or individually. Please request the current price list by writing to:

WORD OF GRACE COMMUNICATIONS
P.O. Box 4000
Panorama City, CA 91412

Or call the following toll-free number:
1-800-55-GRACE

1
The Power of the Word
in the Believer's Life—Part 1

Outline

Introduction
A. The Attributes of the Bible
   1. The Bible is infallible
   2. The Bible is inerrant
   3. The Bible is complete
   4. The Bible is authoritative
   5. The Bible is sufficient
     a) Salvation
     b) Perfection
     c) Hope
     d) Blessing
   6. The Bible is effective
   7. The Bible is determinative
B. The Authenticity of the Bible
   1. Experience
   2. Science
     a) Rainfall
     b) Fixed orbits
     c) Balance
   3. Christ
   4. Miracles
   5. Prophecy

Lesson
I. The Source of Truth

II. The Source of Happiness

Introduction

It is vital for every Christian to know how to study the Bible. You should be able to dig into God's Word yourself to glean and to gain all the riches that the

7

Bible contains. I often think of the words of Jeremiah who said, "Thy words were found, and I did eat them, and thy word was unto me the joy and rejoicing of mine heart" (Jer. 15:16*a*). The Word of God is a tremendous resource. Christians should not be handicapped in their own ability to study God's Word for themselves. So we are going to be examining how to study the Bible. But first, we should see *why* it is important to study it.

Walter Scott, a British novelist and poet and a great Christian, was dying when he said to his secretary, "Bring me the Book." His secretary looked at the thousands of books in his library and said, "Dr. Scott, which book?" He said, "The Book, the Bible—the only Book for a dying man." And I would have to add that the Bible is not just the only Book for a *dying* man, but it's the only Book for a *living* man, because it is the Word of life, as well as the hope in death.

So we come to the Word of God with a tremendous sense of excitement and anticipation. But before I share with you how to study the Bible, I must tell you about the authority of the Word of God. Then you will see the importance of Bible study. Also, we must state from the very beginning that the Scripture is the Word of God. It is not man's opinion, it is not human philosophy, it is not somebody's ideas, it is not a pooling of the best thoughts of the best men—it is the Word of God. Consequently, there are several things we need to realize about it.

A. The Attributes of the Bible

1. The Bible is infallible

The Bible, in its entirety, has no mistakes. Specifically, in its original autographs it is without errors. In Psalm 19:7 the Bible says of itself, "The law of the Lord is perfect." It is flawless because it was authored by God—and He is flawless. Therefore, if God wrote the Bible, and if He is the ultimate authority, and if His character is flawless, then the Bible is flawless and is the ultimate authority. You see, the fact that God is perfect demands that the original autograph, the original giving of the Word of God, must also be perfect. So, the Bible is infallible, and that's the first reason to study it; it is the only Book that never makes a mistake—everything it says is the truth.

Not only is it *infallible,* but there's a second word we use in describing the Bible, and that is:

2. The Bible is inerrant

The Bible is not only infallible in total, but inerrant in its parts. In Proverbs 30:5-6 it says, "Every word of God is pure. . . . Add thou not unto his words, lest he reprove thee, and thou be found a liar." So every Word of God is pure and true.

The Bible is not only *infallible* and *inerrant,* but:

3. The Bible is complete

Nothing needs to be added. Now that may be a surprise to some people, because there are those today who believe we need to add to the Bible. There exists a philosophy/theology combination known as neoorthodoxy. It tells us that the Bible was simply a comment in its day on man's spiritual experiences, and today man is still having spiritual experiences, therefore he needs another comment. One writer said that we need a Bible to be written today, just as we did when the Bible we have in our hands was written, because we need somebody to comment on what God is doing now. He also said that when Tom or Mary stand up in your church and say, "Thus says the Lord," they are as equally inspired as Isaiah, Jeremiah, or any of the other prophets (J. Rodman Williams, *The Era of the Spirit,* Logos International, 1971). In other words, they claim that the Bible is not complete. That's the current philosophical/theological thought. Let's look at the end of the last book of the Bible, the book of Revelation: "If any man shall add unto these things, God shall add unto him the plagues that are written in this book; and if any man shall take away from the words of the book of this prophecy, God shall take away his part from the tree of life, and out of the holy city, and from the things which are written in this book" (22:18*b*-19). The Bible ends with a warning not to take away anything, and not to add anything. That's a testimony of its completeness. It is *infallible* in its total, *inerrant* in its parts, and it is *complete.*

A fourth way to describe the Bible's attributes is to say that:

4. The Bible is authoritative

If it is perfect and complete, then it is the last Word—the final authority. Isaiah 1:2 says, "Hear, O heavens, and give ear, O earth; for the Lord hath spoken." When God speaks everybody listens, because His is the final authority; the Bible demands obedience. We can discuss its implications, its applications, and its meanings, but we shouldn't discuss whether or not it is true.

In John 8 Jesus was confronted by some of the Jewish leaders, and there were other people present. Verses 30*b*-31 say, "Many believed on him. Then said Jesus to those Jews who believed on Him, If ye continue in my word, then are ye my disciples indeed." In other words, He demanded response to His Word. It is *authoritative.* In Galatians 3:10 it says, "Cursed is everyone that continueth not in all things which are written in the book of the law, to do them." Amazing! Cursed was anyone who didn't continue in everything that was written in the law. That's a tremendous claim to absolute authority. In James 2:9-10 we read, "But if ye have respect of persons, ye commit sin, and are convicted of the law as transgressors. For whosoever shall keep the whole law, and yet offend in one point, he is guilty of all." To violate the Bible at one point is to break God's law. The Bible is *authoritative* in every part.

Well, the Bible is *infallible, inerrant, complete, authoritative,* and:

5. The Bible is sufficient

The Bible is sufficient for a number of things:

a) Salvation

In 2 Timothy 3:15 Paul said to Timothy, "And that from a child thou hast known the holy scriptures, which are able to make thee wise unto salvation through faith which is in Christ Jesus." First of all, the Bible is *sufficient* to make you wise unto salvation. Ask yourself this question: What is more important than salvation? Nothing! It is the greatest reality in the universe—and the Bible reveals that salvation.

b) Perfection

Verse 16 of 2 Timothy 3 says, "All scripture is given by inspiration of God, and is profitable *for doctrine*"—that means "teaching, principles of wisdom, divine standards, or divine truths"; *"for reproof"*—that means you're able to go to someone and say, "Hey, you're out of line. You can't behave like that; there's a standard and you're not keeping it." Scripture is also profitable *"for correction"*—that says to the person you've just reproved, "Now don't do that, do this instead; this is the right path." You teach, you reprove, you show the correct way—and further it is profitable *"for instruction in righteousness."* Now you point to the new way and show them how to walk in it. The Bible is a fantastic Book. It can take somebody who doesn't know God, who isn't saved, and then save them. Then it will teach them, reprove them when they do wrong, point out the right thing to do, and then show them how to walk in that right path.

The result is stated in verse 17: "That the man of God may be perfect, thoroughly furnished unto all good works." The incredible reality of the Bible is that it is *sufficient* to do the whole job.

c) Hope

In Romans 15:4 it says, "For whatever things were written in earlier times [referring to the Bible] were written for our learn-

10

ing, that we, through patience and comfort of the scriptures, might have hope." The Bible is the source of patience and comfort, ultimately giving us hope now and forever.

d) Blessing

I think of the tremendous text of James 1:25, "But whosoever looketh into the perfect law of liberty (the Scripture), and continueth in it, he being not a forgetful hearer but a doer of the work, this man shall be blessed in his deed." That's great! When you read it and then do it—you're blessed. Back in verse 21, James says that we should "receive with meekness the engrafted word, which is able to save your souls." The Greek text literally means it is able to "save your life." In other words, it will save your life if you receive the Word of God. I think by that he means that it will give you the fullest life imaginable. But it is possible also for a Christian that doesn't obey the Word of God to lose his life. In 1 Corinthians 11 some of the Christians in Corinth violated the Lord's Table, and He took them home. Verse 30 says, "For this cause many are weak and sickly among you, and many sleep." Ananias and Sapphira disobeyed God's command and dropped dead in front of the whole church (Acts 5:1-11). So James said, "If you receive the engrafted (implanted) Word, and you obey it, and you continue in it, it has an incredible way of perfecting you, of blessing you, of saving your life." All these things are true of the Word of God.

6. The Bible is effective

Listen to the words of Isaiah 55:11: "So shall my word be that goeth forth out of my mouth; it shall not return unto me void, but it shall accomplish that which I please." That's great! God's Word is effective. One of the incredible things about being a teacher of the Word of God is that it will do what it says it will do.

Is your product always effective?

I often wonder about the door-to-door salesman who tries to demonstrate his product, and then it doesn't work right. I always remember the lady who lived in the country, and a vacuum cleaner salesman came by with a high-pressure sales pitch. He said, "Hey, lady, I've got the greatest product you've ever seen. This vacuum cleaner will eat up anything. In fact, if I don't control it, it will suck up your carpet." Before she could say anything, he said, "Lady, I want to give you a demonstration." He immediately went to the fireplace and threw some of

11

the ashes in the middle of the carpet. He also had a bag of stuff which he dumped on the carpet. Then he said, "I want you to watch it suck every bit of that up." Well, she was just standing there aghast. Finally, he said to her, "Lady, if it doesn't suck up every bit of this, I'll eat it all with a spoon." She looked him right in the eyes and said, "Well sir, start eating, because we ain't got no electricity."

Now it's pretty tough to be caught in a situation where your product doesn't work. But that never happens with the Bible—it is always effective—it always does exactly what it says it will do. That's a tremendous reality about the Scripture.

In 1 Thessalonians 1:5 we see a great verse about the effectiveness of the Scripture: "For our gospel came not unto you in word only, but also in power, and in the Holy Spirit, and in much assurance." In other words, when you hear the Word of God, it isn't just words. When the Word goes forth it has power; it is powered by the Holy Spirit, and we have the assurance that it will do what it says.

Well, what have we said so far? We have seen that the Word of God is *infallible* in total, *inerrant* in its parts, *complete* so that nothing is to be diminished or added to it, *authoritative* so that whatever it says is absolutely true and commands our obedience, *sufficient* so that it is able to do to us and for us everything we need, and *effective*—it will do exactly what it says it will do. Finally:

7. The Bible is determinative

The Bible is determinative because how you respond to the Word of God determines the essence of your life and your eternal destiny. In John 8:47 Jesus said, "He that is of God heareth God's words; ye, therefore, hear them not, because ye are not of God." In other words, the determination of whether an individual is of God or not of God is based on whether he listens to the Word of God. First Corinthians 2:9 says, "Eye hath not seen, nor ear heard, neither have entered into the heart of man, the things which God hath prepared for them that love him." Man could never conceive of God's dominion on his own. Man could never conceive that he would be a part of it. Man could never conceive in his own humanness, in his own patterns of logic, all that God has prepared for him. But verses 10-12 say, "But God hath revealed them unto us by His Spirit; for the Spirit searcheth all things, yea, the deep things of God. For what man knoweth the things of a man, except the spirit of man which is in him? Even so the things of God knoweth no man, but the Spirit of God. Now we have received, not the spirit of the world, but the Spirit who is of God; that we might know the things that are freely given to us of God." Then verse 14 says, "But the natural man receiveth not the things of the Spirit of God." Now there are two kinds of people: the people who receive the things of God, and the people who do not—the people who can receive, and the people who cannot. The unbelieving people can't receive it because they don't have the Holy Spirit. But the people who know God have the Holy Spirit, and they receive the Word of God. You see, it's a determiner. Those people who receive the Word of God indicate by their understanding of it that they possess the Holy Spirit—and that proves that they are believers.

I remember talking to a man who continually admitted that he didn't understand the Bible. But he couldn't because he didn't have the one thing necessary to understand it—the indwelling of the Holy Spirit in his soul. So, the beauty, glory, and capabilities of the Word of God are presented to us in these simple words: it is *infallible, inerrant, complete, authoritative, sufficient, effective,* and *determinative.* Now somebody might come along and say, "Well, that's really great that the Bible makes all those claims for itself. If all of this is true then I've got to find out about those principles. But how can I really be sure that it's true?"

B. The Authenticity of the Bible

There are five basic areas that prove that the Bible is true. The first area is:

1. Experience

I believe the Bible is true because it gives us the experience that it claims it will give us. For example, the Bible says that God will forgive our sin (1 John 1:9). I believe that. I accepted His forgiveness, and you know what? He did it. But you may say, "How do you know that?" Because I have a sense of freedom from guilt; I have a sense of forgiveness. The Bible says that "if any man be in Christ, he is a new creation; old things are passed away; behold, all things are become new" (2 Cor. 5:17). I came to Jesus Christ one day, and do you know what happened? Old things passed away and all things became new, and I experienced it. The Bible changes lives. Someone said that a Bible that's falling apart usually belongs to somebody who isn't. That's true because the Bible can put lives together. Millions of people all over the world are living proof that the Bible is true. They've experienced it.

Although that's a great argument in one sense, it's a weak one in another sense, because if you start basing everything on experience, you're going to run into some people who have had some pretty wild experiences: the drunk who sees pink elephants, but really doesn't or the one who sits under a tree and contemplates his navel—and whoever else. They're going to have an experience, but if you base it all on experience you're going to have problems. So, that's just one way of the five, and it's probably the poorest way, but it's still evidence for some.

A second thing that proves the validity of the Bible is:

2. Science

Some people say, "Well, the Bible is not a science book; it's scientifically incorrect, and it doesn't use scientific language. Why does the Old Testament say that the sun stood still? Now we know that the sun didn't stand still. In fact, in the old times they thought the sun was going around the earth instead of vice-versa. That's just a typical biblical flaw." But what happened is that the earth stopped revolving, and it *appeared* that the sun stood still (Josh. 10:13). You see, some people try to analyze the statement scientifically, but they just see what *appeared* to have happened. We all do the same thing. When you get up in the morning and look toward the east, you don't say, "Oh my, what a lovely earth rotation." No, you call it a sunrise, and you understand what you're saying. Likewise, you don't look to the west and say, "What a lovely earth rotation." No, it's a sunset. When someone asks you if you'd like another helping at dinner, you could say, "Well, gastronomical satiety admonishes me that I have arrived at a state of deglutition consistent with dietetic integrity." Or you could say, "No, thanks, I've had enough." You see, you don't always need a scientific answer for everything. Sometimes, just pure observation is sufficient. The Bible says some things that are from the viewpoint of human observation, but on the other hand, whenever the Bible speaks about a scientific principle, it is dead accurate. In fact, let's examine three areas the Bible addresses more closely.

a) Rainfall

In Isaiah 55:10 it says, "For as the rain cometh down, and the snow from heaven, and returneth not there, but watereth the earth, and maketh it bring forth and bud, that it may give seed to the sower, and bread to the eater." Isaiah spoke centuries before the hydrological cycle was ever discovered. He said, "The rain and the snow comes down and don't return again until they have watered the earth." But it's only been in modern times that hydrology has been understood. That is what happens: the rain falls down on the land, it waters the land, it runs off into the streams, down to the rivers, into the sea, and from the sea it returns again to the clouds; then it is taken over the land and dropped again. The ever constant hydrological cycle, and Isaiah 55:10 laid it out.

Now some might say, "Well, a blind pig can find the slop once in a while—maybe Isaiah just took a lucky guess." That might have been a possibility if it weren't for the fact that the same thing is discussed in several other portions of the Bible. Job 36:27-29 comments, "For he maketh small the drops of water; they pour down rain according to their vapor, which the clouds do drop and distill upon man abundantly. Also can any understand the spreadings of the clouds, or the noise of his tabernacle?" Once again a discussion of rain. Compare also what it says in Psalm 135:7: "He causeth the vapors to ascend from the ends of the earth; he maketh lightnings for the rain; he bringeth the wind out of his treasuries." Another discussion of this wonderful sequence of rain and the ascending vapors from the sea to plant the water again in the clouds.

b) Fixed orbits

The Bible also comments on the fixed orbits of the heavenly bodies. Jeremiah 31:35-36 (NASB*) discusses this, and Psalm 19 also talks about it. I really feel that as you get into the Bible you will find incredible things about science that reveal the truthfulness of God's Word. You never need to be ashamed of the Bible. You're never going to run into a problem in the Bible which you can't solve in one of two ways: first, by looking through the rest of the Bible and understanding how to interpret it; second, by realizing that you're never going to understand it until you meet God. There are some things we don't understand or know, but the truth is that we're not going to run into an error in the Scripture—not even scientifically.

c) Balance

Within the science of geology there is a study called *isostasy,* which is fairly new. Isostasy is the study of the balance of the earth, and it says that equal weights are necessary to support equal weights. So, land mass must be supported equally by water mass. But they really haven't discovered anything actually new. If we go back to good old Isaiah again, who was

New American Standard Bible.

15

not a scientist but simply a prophet of God, we find in Isaiah 40:12 that it says: "Who hath measured the waters in the hollow of his hand, and measured out heaven with the span, and measured the dust of the earth in a measure, and weighed the mountains in scales, and the hills in a balance?" God knew all about isostasy. It's just incredible when you come to the Bible and start to study it even scientifically.

They said of Herbert Spencer, who died in 1903, that he had discovered the greatest thing about the categorizing of all things that exist in the environment of the universe. He said everything could fall into these categories: time, force, action, space, and matter. Five classic scientific categories, and he said everything fit into those categories. The world hailed him as a great scientist, a great man of discovery. But do you want to know something? All five of those categories are in the first verse of the Bible: "In the beginning (that's time) God (that's force) created (that's action) the heaven (that's space) and the earth (that's matter). Genesis 1:1 shows us that when the Bible speaks, it speaks accurately. So, science is a good way to show the authority and the validity of Scripture.

Another area of tremendous evidence for the truth of the Bible is the very life of:

3. Christ

I could give you several reasons that this is true, but for now let me suggest just one: Jesus Himself believed in the authority of the Bible. In Matthew 5:18 Jesus says, "Till heaven and earth pass, one jot or one tittle shall in no way pass from the law till all be fulfilled." Furthermore, He showed His trust in the authority of Scripture by quoting from every part of the Old Testament. Jesus believed in the absolute inspired authority of the Word of God.

The fourth area of proof that the Bible is true is the area of:

4. Miracles

The Bible is a divine Book because it has miracles; and that proves that God is involved in it. It's got to be a supernatural Book because of all the supernatural activity it contains. Now some might say, "Well, how do you know all the miracles are true?" Because miracles are given in Scripture and there is supportive information. For example, when Jesus rose from the dead, more than five hundred people saw Him after the resurrection. Those are enough witnesses to convince any jury. The miraculous nature of the Bible speaks of God.

So experience, science, the testimony of Christ, and the miracles of the Bible all prove that Scripture is true. Then fifth, there is:

5. Prophecy

There is no way to explain the fact that the Bible predicts things that are going to happen historically, unless we see God as the Author. Peter Stoner, in his book *Science Speaks,* said that if you just take a few prophecies (he's a scientist dealing in the science of mathematical probability, and he selected three or four prophecies from the Old Testament), and if you just add up the probabilities that these three or four things could come to pass by accident, it would be one chance in two quintillion that such an accident could happen—and yet every detail has come to pass. One chance in two quintillion would be like filling the state of Texas thirty-five-feet deep in silver dollars, putting an "x" on one of them, and giving a blind man one pick. He'd have one chance in two quintillion in picking the one with an "x" on it. That's how much chance there is, according to the mathematics of probability, of these three or four prophecies (with their specific details) ever coming to pass by accident. That's incredible! When the Bible speaks prophetically it is right, and it contains literally hundreds of fulfilled prophecies.

So we can look at experience, science, Christ, miracles, and fulfilled prophecy to see that the Bible is true. It's an incredible Book—the greatest treasure imaginable.

The Bible is God's holy Word; it's a tremendous resource. But the Christian who never approaches it with an intense commitment to study it is forfeiting a tremendous blessing. So now I want to give you six areas that appear as major benefits to start with, because these are the things that are going to become your motivation.

Lesson

I. The Source of Truth

In John 17:17b Jesus prayed to the Father and said, "Thy word is truth." That's a great statement, but do you realize what it is to have the truth? Quite often when I confront people about Jesus Christ they say, "But I don't know what the truth is." Even Pilate came to the place in his life when he looked at Jesus and said, "What is truth?" (John 18:38a). Many people have that same thought; nevertheless, we're in a world that searches for truth.

It is said that nearly three thousand new pages of material are printed every sixty seconds in our society today. That is really cranking the information out. But did you know that books don't really work

17

anymore? They're too big. So now we have microfilm, microfiche, and other tiny things they put information on. In fact, I saw a tiny chip that had the entire 66 books of the Bible on it. People are working on those kinds of things because we've got to reduce storage factors so we can keep all this information. (I'm not sure we ought to bother with most of it.) Some people have even said that microfilm is too big. So now they're developing laser storage. They store information, somehow, on a tiny crystal, and every facet of the crystal has information on it. Then they shoot a laser beam on the crystal at just the right point, and it flashes the words they want on a screen. But that's also too bulky, so now they've developed what is known as molecular storage. They say that they will be able to store the entire Library of Congress on an object the size of a sugar cube. Now that's a lot of information (and a lot of misinformation), because our society is chasing truth.

The Bible even says that men are "ever learning, and never able to come to the knowledge of the truth" (2 Tim. 3:7). Do you know what that's like? I remember that when I was in junior high school, I had a terrible time with algebra. I'd go home and work on one of those silly problems for hours. Then I'd go back to school the next day without the answer, and that was so frustrating to me. But you've had that problem too: you've worked on something and never solved it or found the answer. And that's the way it is with people in the world. They read, they study, they think, they reason, they listen, they talk, they interact, and they never get the real truth. They never settle on anything, and the frustration is overwhelming. I remember talking to a man who just kind of left society altogether; he just bailed out and got on drugs. He had graduated from Boston University but he was living in the woods, sleeping in a pup tent. I asked him, "Whatever made you do this?" He said, "Well, I searched for the answer so long, I finally decided to blow my mind on drugs. At least now I don't even have to ask the questions." Now that's the despair of never knowing the truth.

Where is real truth?

The writer Franz Kafka gave a great illustration about education. He pictured a bombed-out city where all that was left was rubble. Everywhere there were people bleeding and dying; there was smoke and smoldering fire—just total rubble. But in the middle of the city was an ivory tower piercing the sky, pristine white, untouched by any bombs. Then, there was this solitary figure winding his way through the rubble. When he got to the tall white building, he walked in and went up to the top story. He came to a dark hall, and at the end of it was a little light. He walked in the darkness until he came to the light, he turned, and walked into a bathroom. Inside sat a man with a fishing pole, fishing in the bathtub. The solitary stranger said to him, "Hey, what are you doing?"

The man said, "I'm fishing."

The stranger looked in the bathtub and said, "There's no fish in the bathtub and there's no water."

The man said, "I know," and kept on fishing.

Kafka said, "That is *higher education*."

You see, man has lost the truth.

It's fantastic to realize, and sometimes I think we forget it, that every time we pick up the Bible, we pick up the truth. What a tremendous legacy we have. But we can't take it for granted, and we certainly can't let it just sit around. So the first reason that I believe we need to study the Word of God is because it is the source of truth. Jesus said, "If ye continue in my word . . . ye shall know the truth, and the truth shall make you free" (John 8:31*b*-32). What did He mean by that? Well, just like the guy who works on a math problem, as soon as he finds the answer—he's free. Just like the scientist in the lab pouring the different solutions into test tubes, he stays with it until he says, "Eureka, I found it!"—then he's free. Man will search and struggle and grapple and grope for the truth until he finds it—then he's free. Listen, one reason to study the Bible is that the truth is there. The truth about God; the truth about man; the truth about life; the truth about death; the truth about you and me; the truth about men, women, children, husbands, wives, dads, and mothers; the truth about friends and enemies; the truth about how you ought to be at work and how you ought to be at home; even the truth about how you ought to eat, drink, how you ought to live, how you ought to think—the truth is all there. What a resource we have. Cherish it.

A second reason that you should want to study the Bible is because it is:

II. The Source of Happiness

Some would rather use "joy" or "blessing," but "happiness" says it. The truth is there and it brings us joy, or happiness. In Psalm 19:8*a* it says, "The statutes of the Lord are right, rejoicing the heart." It's just talking about the principles of the Scripture. When you begin to study the Bible and learn the great truths it contains, you will get excited. I study the Bible a lot because I'm constantly teaching and preaching the Word, but I also study it on my own because I love it so much, and the exhilaration that comes to me in the discovery of great truths in the Word of God has never diminished. The greatest thrill I've known in my life is the tremendous exhilaration that comes to my heart when I have cracked open the shell of an incredible truth in the Word of God. In fact, Proverbs 8:34 says, "Blessed [happy] is the man who heareth me." In Luke 11:28 Jesus says, "Blessed [happy] are they that hear the word of God, and keep it." Do you want to be a happy person? Then obey God's Word.

It's amazing to me how so many people know what the Bible teaches, but they don't obey it—so they forfeit happiness. Some people say, "Well, the book of Revelation is so hard to understand. I study the other stuff, but I don't want to get involved in Revelation." But look at what Revelation 1:3 says: "Blessed is he that readeth, and they that hear the words of this prophecy." The word "blessed" means "happy." Do you want to be happy? Read Revelation. Yes, to be happy, read the Word of God and respond to it. I love 1 John 1:4; it says, "And these things write we unto you, that your joy may be full." Isn't that great? Then there's a wonderful statement made by our Lord in that magnificent fifteenth chapter of John where He presents Himself as the Vine. In verse 11 He says, "These things have I spoken unto you, that my joy might remain in you, and that your joy might be full." What a tremendous thought—joy from the Scripture.

The sensation Scripture creates within us

In Luke 24 Jesus has risen from the dead and He is on His way to Emmaus with the two disciples who don't recognize Him (vv. 13-32). Beginning in verse 24 they tell Jesus, "And certain of those who were with us went to the sepulcher, and found it even as the women had said; but him they saw not. Then he said unto them, O foolish ones, and slow of heart to believe all that the prophets have spoken!" Christ is talking to them, but they don't know who it is. "Ought not Christ to have suffered these things, and to enter into his glory?" After His resurrection, nobody knew who Christ was until He revealed Himself to them. "And beginning at Moses and all the prophets, he expounded unto them, in all the scriptures, the things concerning himself." Jesus taught them through the Scriptures, and they were listening. Then as they had their meal, all of a sudden the light dawned: "And their eyes were opened, and they recognized him; and he vanished out of their sight." Then I love this, "And they said one to another, Did not our heart burn within us, while he talked with us along the way, and while he opened to us the scriptures?" When He opened to them the Scriptures, their hearts literally burned within them.

20

There is joy in the Word of God if you obey it. If you don't keep His Word, then there's no joy. However, I would hasten to add that God is gracious. He doesn't expect us to keep every single principle all the time and never waver, but it is a matter of the attitude of our heart. *If your heart is committed to obeying the Word, then He'll fill your life with joy.* I know that people want to know truth and they want to be happy, especially those of us who are Christians, so there is no excuse for us not knowing the truth and not living lives that are literally filled with exhilaration and joy—we have it available in the Word of God.

Focusing on the Facts

1. Why is the Bible the only Book for a living man as well as a dying man (see p. 8)?

2. How can we know that the Bible is infallible in its original autographs (see p. 8)?

3. What word describes that the Bible is true in its parts (see p. 8)?

4. What passage of the Bible is a testimony to its completeness (see p. 9)?

5. Why does the Bible demand obedience (see p. 9)?

6. Give some verses that support the authority of the Bible (see pp. 9-10).

7. What things is the Bible sufficient for? Explain (see pp. 10-11).

8. What is Scripture profitable for? Explain (2 Tim. 3:16; see p. 10).

9. According to James 1:21, what is the Word of God able to do when you receive it (see p. 11)?

10. What does Isaiah 55:11 indicate about the Bible (see p. 11)?

11. Explain how the Bible is determinative. How are believers able to understand the Word of God? Why can't unbelievers understand it (1 Cor. 2:9-14; see pp. 12-13)?

12. Explain how experience is able to prove that the Bible is true. What is the weakness in using experience as proof (see pp. 13-14)?

13. What are three areas of science that the Bible discusses (see pp. 14-16)?

14. How does the Bible support the scientific principle of hydrology (Isa. 55:10; see pp. 14-15)?

15. What is the study of isostasy? What does the Bible say about it (Isa. 40:12; see pp. 15-16)?

16. What five classic scientific categories are found in the first verse of the Bible (see p. 16)?

17. How did Jesus Christ reveal His trust in the authority of Scripture (see p. 16)?

18. How can we know that all the miracles recorded in the Bible are true (see pp. 16-17)?

19. What is the only way to explain how the Bible could predict historical events accurately (see p. 17)?

20. What verse in the Bible indicates that God's Word is the source of truth (see p. 17)?

21. What did Jesus mean when He said, "If ye continue in my word . . . ye shall know the truth, and the truth shall make you free" (John 8:31-32; see p. 19)?

22. What are some of the truths that are found in the Bible (see p. 19)?

23. Since the Bible is the source of truth, what does it give to the one who believes it (Ps. 19:8; see pp. 19-20)?

24. How can you be a happy person (see p. 20)?

Pondering the Principles

1. Read 2 Timothy 3:16-17. In what ways has the Bible been profitable to you in teaching you doctrine? In what ways have others used Scripture to reprove you? In what ways have others used it to correct your spiritual walk? How have others used the Bible to train you in righteousness? Just as others have had the opportunity to use the Bible to move you along the path of perfection, look for opportunities to be used of God in the same way in another person's life.

2. Read 1 Corinthians 2:9-12. How are Christians able to know spiritual truth? Take this time to thank God for your salvation, and that because of your salvation, you can learn spiritual truth. Ask Him to give you greater insight into His Word. But just as you want to learn more from Him, He wants a greater commitment on your part to study His Word. Make that commitment by setting aside a specific time each day to study God's Word.

3. Read Psalm 19:7-11. According to those verses, what are the benefits of God's Word? In what ways has each of those benefits been manifest in your life? Be specific. How desirous are you of studying God's Word? According to verse 11, what is the result of obeying God's Word? As a result of this study, how has your attitude changed regarding your Bible study? What changes will you implement to get more out of your study?

2
The Power of the Word
in the Believer's Life—Part 2

Outline

Review
I. The Source of Truth
II. The Source of Happiness

Lesson
A. Legal Obedience
B. Gracious Obedience
  1. Commitment reduced (John 21:1-14)
  2. Commitment revealed (John 21:15-17)
  3. Commitment required
  4. Commitment rewarded
III. The Source of Victory
A. Victory over Satan (Matt. 4:1-11)
  1. Verses 1-2
  2. Verses 3-4
  3. Verses 5-7
  4. Verses 8-11
B. Victory over Demons (Luke 4:33-36)
C. Victory over Temptation (Eph. 6:17)
IV. The Source of Growth
A. Prerequisites for Growth
  1. Sanctification
  2. Study
B. Patterns of Growth (1 John 2:13-14)
  1. Little children
  2. Young men
  3. Fathers
V. The Source of Power
A. Hebrews 4:12
B. Romans 1:16
C. Ephesians 4:23
D. Romans 12:2*b*

    E. 2 Corinthians 3:18

    F. Ephesians 1:3—3:12

VI. The Source of Guidance

Conclusion
1. Believe it
2. Honor it
3. Love it
4. Obey it
5. Fight for it
6. Preach it
7. Study it

Review

We have said that we should study the Bible because it is:

I. The Source of Truth (see pp. 17-19)

II. The Source of Happiness (see pp. 19-21)

We should study the Bible not only because it is the source of truth, but also because it is the source of happiness or joy. Jesus, in Luke 11:28, says, "Blessed [happy] are they that hear the word of God, and keep [obey] it." Now when we talk about obeying the Word of God we need to differentiate between two kinds of obedience: first, legal obedience, and second, gracious obedience.

Lesson

A. Legal Obedience

Legal obedience, or we could better call it legalistic obedience, pertains to the "covenant of works," the "old covenant," or the "Mosaic covenant." Legalistic obedience demands absolute, perfect obedience without a single failure (Gal. 3:10). If you fail, that's the end. One false move and you're finished. Now that's legal obedience. This is the "covenant of works," but in contrast to that in the Scripture, we have the "covenant of grace."

B. Gracious Obedience

Gracious obedience pertains to a loving, gracious, merciful, and forgiving attitude on the part of God. Legalistic obedience says you had better keep every rule or you're finished. Gracious obedience says if God sees in your heart a spirit of grace; if He sees a sincere and loving and humble willingness to obey; if He sees a positive response to His Word, even though there are times when

24

we fail, then He counts us as obedient because that's the spirit in our hearts. Even though our gracious obedience may be filled with defects, it's the proper attitude that God is after. That's a tremendous principle, and I want to illustrate it for you because it's so important.

1. Commitment reduced (John 21:1-14)

A favorite passage of mine, John 21, graphically illustrates several spiritual truths. It's all about Peter, who had gone fishing when he shouldn't have. The Lord had already called him into the ministry, but he went fishing instead and violated the Lord's call. He and some of the other disciples were fishing, but they didn't catch any fish. They had fished all night, but it was totally fruitless. When morning came, Jesus appeared on the shore and asked them if they had caught anything. Peter, like the rest, had nothing to show. It was a great lesson for them because God was saying, "If you think you can go back to fishing, you're wrong. You've been called to the ministry, so your fishing is finished. I can reroute every fish in every sea you approach." So Jesus called them over for breakfast.

2. Commitment revealed (John 21:15-17)

The Lord had made breakfast, and I imagine He made breakfast like He made anything: "Breakfast!"—and there it was. After they had eaten, verse 15 says, "Jesus saith to Simon Peter, Simon, son of Jonah, lovest thou me more than these?" Now that was an interesting statement. Jesus used the most grandiose word for "love" that was in the Greek language, *agapaō* from which we get the word *agapē.*

In other words, Jesus said, "Do you super love Me? Do you love Me to the limit of love?" Peter responded, "I sure like You a lot." Peter used a different word that spoke of a lesser love, *phileō.* And the Lord said, "Feed My lambs." The second time Jesus said to Peter, "Peter, do you super love Me?" Peter replied, "Well Lord, I like You a lot." Jesus said, "Feed my sheep" (v. 16). Do you know why Peter kept saying, "I like You a lot," instead of the word Jesus used? Simple. His life didn't match such a claim. He knew if he said, "Lord, I super love You," Jesus would have said, "Oh, is that why you don't obey? Have you forgotten that I told you a long time ago that if you love Me you'll keep My commandments? How could you say you super love Me when you don't even do what I say?" Peter wasn't about to get himself in that trap, so he said, "I like You a lot."

"He saith unto him the third time, Simon, son of Jonah, lovest thou me?" (v. 17). Jesus said, "Peter, do you like Me a lot?" Now that hurt. You see, Peter thought he was being fair; he wasn't even going to claim super love, but Jesus questioned the love that Peter did claim. The verse continues, "Peter was grieved because he said unto him the third time, Lovest thou me? (Do you like Me a lot?) And he said unto him, Lord, thou knowest all things; thou knowest that I love thee." Peter said, "Lord, You know everything, You know I like You a lot." He appealed to the doctrine of omniscience. He wanted Jesus to read his heart because his love wasn't obvious from his life. The doctrine of omniscience is a great reality, but when I was a kid I thought it was bad; I thought God was going around spying on everybody. Now I realize that if God wasn't omniscient there would be plenty of days that he wouldn't know that I loved Him because it wouldn't be obvious from my life. So Peter says, "Lord, You know everything—You know that I love You."

3. Commitment required

And do you know what the Lord Jesus told Peter? The Lord is so good. He looked at that disciple who couldn't even claim the supreme love, that one who couldn't even obey, that one who couldn't even stay awake at a prayer meeting, that one who stuck his foot in his mouth every time he had an opportunity, that one who almost drowned when he could have walked on water, that one who wanted to tell Jesus not to go to the cross, that one who grabbed a sword and tried to chop up the Roman army, and Jesus said to that character who had fouled up almost every opportunity he had, "You're My man." Three times He said, "Feed my lambs. . . . feed my sheep. . . . feed my sheep" (vv. 15-17). Jesus took Peter on the basis of his heart attitude of willingness to obey, even though he blundered. God works with us on the premise of gracious obedience—not legal obedience. Here was a man who failed to obey over and over again, but in his heart he really wanted to do it. The spirit was willing, but the flesh was weak. The Lord Jesus knew that, and that's how God looks at us. He says, "My Word is the source of joy if you obey it, and if you obey My Word, I'll fill your life with joy." No, He doesn't mean that if you ever fail one little bit in His rules, that's the end of joy, and then you have misery. Instead, He says, "If I read as an attitude of your heart a style of life that shows a commitment and the desire to obey, I will pass over those failures." It's the deep commitment He's after, and that's the source of joy.

4. Commitment rewarded

As you study the Word and hear what it says, and you draw out its principles and obey those principles because it's in your heart to obey them, then God pours out the blessing and joy. But if you crank out obedience in every legalistic manner possible, and if in your heart you don't want to do it, He will never give you the joy. To do good deeds without the right heart attitude doesn't count. Let me show you what I mean. The Bible talks about different kinds of fruit, and it talks about the fruit of the Spirit. Before there's ever fruit in your life, such as winning people to Christ, and before the fruit on the outside means anything, it has to come from the fruit of the Spirit on the inside. Action fruit, things you do without the proper attitude fruit, is pure legalism—Pharisaism. If you crank out all the stuff you want to on the outside and you are a legalist to the teeth like the Pharisees, then you'll never know joy. On the other hand, if you have a heart of obedience with the right attitude, even though you may fail on the outside, God will give you joy because He sees the gracious, obedient spirit in your heart. That's what He desires.

So, why should we study the Bible? Number one, it's the source of truth, and number two, it's the source of rejoicing.

I study the Bible, but I've got problems

One thing we must realize is that God doesn't tell us exactly when we're going to get the joy—we might have to wait a little while. In John 16 Jesus said to the disciples, "I'm leaving" (v. 16). Well, they just sat there moping because they had put all their proverbial eggs in one basket. Everybody had left his trade and had been following Jesus for three years. Then Jesus said, "One day soon I'm going to leave, guys." They all thought, "Now wait a minute—we joined this deal thinking the kingdom was going to come. What's wrong?" They were very sorrowful, so Jesus says in John 16:20, "Verily, verily, I say unto you, Ye shall weep and lament, but the world shall rejoice; and ye shall be sorrowful, but your sorrow shall be turned into joy." In other words, "You've got to realize that sometimes there's going to be sorrow before there's ever going to be joy." In fact, if we didn't know sorrow, we wouldn't understand joy when it came. If we didn't know pain, we wouldn't know pleasure.

I read an interesting article that said the difference between an itch and a tickle cannot be defined medically. Yet, a tickle is something that makes you happy, and an itch is something that irritates. The difference between pleasure and pain can be a very fine line. For example, sometimes there's nothing more wonderful than a real hot shower, but you have to ease in because of the pain; then all of a sudden—ahhh!—the thin line between pain and pleasure. If we didn't know pain we wouldn't know the joy that pleasure could bring. I think one of the reasons God allows sorrow in our lives is so we will understand joy when it comes. Listen, if we obey the Word of God, He'll give us that joy. Maybe not instantaneously when we want it, but always when we need it. I'll tell you, no matter what happens in my life, externally and circumstantially, when I study the Word of God, there's an exhilaration and a joy that is untouched by any circumstance.

A third motivating force, and the third reason to study the Bible, is that the Word is:

III. The Source of Victory

I don't know about you, but I like to win—I don't like to lose. I lose a lot, but I don't like it. I figure if you're going to do something, do it all the way. My dad used to say to me from the time I was a kid, "Listen, Johnny, if you're going to do it, do it to the best of your ability, or it isn't worth doing." I grew up that way, striving for excellence. I see that also in my Christian life. I don't like to give an occasion to the adversary. I don't like to give him an "advantage" over me, as it says in Corinthians (2 Cor. 2:11). I don't like to see Satan victorious; I don't like to see the world master me; I don't like to see the flesh override my spirit—I want to win. I remember my football coach giving us the typical Knute Rockne lecture saying, "You can't be beat, if you won't be beat." I guess we ought to be like that as Christians. There's no reason to give in to the enemy, because as you study the Bible, you'll find out that the Word of God becomes the source of victory.

We would do well to remember what David said: "Thy word have I hidden in mine heart, that I might not sin against thee" (Ps. 119:11). The Word, then, is the source of victory over sin. As the Word of God is taken in, it becomes the resource which the Holy Spirit uses to direct us. We have no way of preventing ourselves from being led into sin, unless the Word of God is there so that it can be brought into our conscious mind. Let me give you something basic to understand: You'll never function on what you don't know. We'll never be able to operate on a principle we never knew. We'll never be able to apply a truth we haven't discovered. So as we feed into our minds the Word of God, it becomes the resource by which the Spirit of God directs and guides. Now let's look at some specific examples of the Word's effectiveness.

A. Victory over Satan (Matt. 4:1-11)

1. Verses 1-2

Here is the classic illustration of facing Satan with the Word of God. It says in verse 1, "Then was Jesus led up by the Spirit into the wilderness to be tested [or tempted] by the devil." As far as God was concerned it was a test because He knew He wouldn't fail; as far as Satan was concerned it was a temptation because he hoped He would fail. The Greek word *peirasmos* can mean either "temptation" or "testing." It's a neutral word that can mean good or bad. From Satan's viewpoint, he wanted it to be bad; from God's viewpoint, He knew that it would be good. So the Spirit led Him into the wilderness knowing He'd pass the test, but Satan was there waiting for Him, hoping He'd fail.

"And when he had fasted forty days and forty nights, he was afterward hungry" (v. 2). That's not surprising, but it's interesting as we remember that Jesus was a perfect human being, without sin; therefore, His body must have had powers beyond anything we could ever experience. It's really amazing to realize that He was not appreciably hungry for those forty days until afterwards, when He knew the gnawing pangs of hunger.

2. Verses 3-4

Finally after forty days, "when the tempter came to him, he said, If thou be the Son of God, command that these stones be made bread." What he's really saying to Jesus is this: "Listen, You're the Son of God, You deserve better than this; what are You doing out here in this wretched wilderness? What are You doing out here starving to death? You're the Son of God, grab some satisfaction, make some bread, You deserve it." Satan was really tempting Him to go against God's plan—to grab His own satisfaction. He was saying, "Do Your own thing—don't depend on God; He hasn't met Your need."

Satan was really tempting Jesus to distrust the care of God. "But he answered and said, It is written, Man shall not live by bread alone, but by every word that proceedeth out of the

29

mouth of God." The Lord quoted Deuteronomy 8:3. In other words, He said, "God promised to care for Me, so I'll keep My trust in that promise, and I'll never use My own powers to violate the promise of God." Jesus countered Satan's temptation with the Word of God.

3. Verses 5-7

"Then the devil taketh him up into the holy city (Jerusalem), and setteth him on a pinnacle of the temple." This was probably the protruding strut that stuck out over the Valley of Hinnom, which may have been a three-hundred-foot drop. Satan said, "Cast thyself down"—and then he quoted Scripture: "He shall give his angels charge concerning thee, and in their hands they shall bear thee up, lest at any time thou dash thy foot against a stone." He said, "If You want to trust God, if You're going to believe God, well, why don't You really believe God and take a swan dive off here and see if He fulfills His Word?" However, "Jesus said unto him, It is written again, Thou shalt not put the Lord, thy God, to the test." In other words, Jesus said, "You don't presume on God." When you believe Him to care for you on a trip, you don't lie in the freeway. There's a difference between trust and presumption.

4. Verses 8-11

Satan then took Jesus to a high mountain and showed Him the kingdoms of the world. He said, "All these things will I give thee, if thou wilt fall down and worship me. Then saith Jesus unto him, Begone, Satan; for it is written, Thou shalt worship the Lord, thy God, and him only shalt thou serve. Then the devil leaveth him, and, behold, angels came and ministered unto him." God fulfilled all His promises. The point is this: Jesus answered the temptation of Satan three times, and every time He quoted directly out of the Old Testament. Listen, as a Christian, it is the capturing of biblical truth in our conscious mind that gives us the capacity to defeat Satan. We can't do it on our own. Jesus literally triumphed over the devil through the Word of God—it is the source of victory. But it's just incredible that people still imagine they can argue Satan out of his temptation of their own logic. It can't be done. Only God's Word gives us victory.

B. Victory over Demons (Luke 4:33-36)

Here we have another interesting illustration, beginning in verse 33: "And in the synagogue there was a man, who had a spirit of an unclean demon, and cried out with a loud voice, saying, Let us alone; what have we to do with thee, thou Jesus of Nazareth? Art thou come to destroy us? I know thee, who thou art: the Holy One of God. And Jesus rebuked him, saying, Hold thy peace, and come out of him. And when the demon had thrown him down in the midst, he came out of him, and hurt him not. And they were all amazed, and spoke among themselves, saying, What a word is this! For with authority and power he commandeth the unclean spirits, and they come out." Do you know what Jesus did there? He once again established His authority and power over Satan with His Word. With one word He just vanquished a legion of demons. The people recognized that Jesus spoke as a man of authority, not like the scribes and the Pharisees. Listen, the Word of Jesus Christ is absolutely authoritative. So, when you know the Word of God, you'll know victory.

C. Victory over Temptation (Eph. 6:17)

In Ephesians chapter 6, Paul's discussion of the armor of the Christian, we find that it finishes with a great piece of armor: "And take the helmet of salvation, and the sword of the Spirit, which is the word of God." This is a tremendous text. He says the final piece of armor is "the sword of the Spirit, which is the word of God." Now when we think of a sword, we usually think of a long thing that someone flails around. The Greek word for that type of sword is *rhomphaia.* But the Greek word used here is *machaira,* which refers to a short, small dagger. The sword of the Spirit, therefore, is not a huge sword that you just flail around, hoping that you'll whack off the head of a demon sooner or later. It is not something you use indiscriminately or wildly. But the sword of the Spirit is a *machaira;* it is a dagger, it is incisive, it must hit a vulnerable spot or it doesn't do any damage. The sword of the Spirit is not something general, but specific.

Now notice further, the Greek word used for "word" in this verse is not *logos. Logos* is a general word: the Bible is the *logos,* Christ is the *logos,* or a general "word" is *logos.* When the Bible wants to speak of a specific, it uses the word *rhema.* Now it means "a specific statement." So the sword of the Spirit is the specific statement of the Word of God that meets the specific point of temptation. Now some people may say, "Well, I have the sword of the Spirit—I own a Bible." Listen, you could own a Bible warehouse, and you wouldn't have the sword of the Spirit. *Having the sword of the Spirit is not owning a Bible, but knowing the specific principle in the Bible that applies to the specific point of temptation.* The only way Christians will know victory in the Christian life is for them to know the principles of the Word of God so that they can apply them to the specific points where Satan attacks, where the flesh attacks, and where the world attacks. As Christians fill themselves up with the Word of God, it then becomes the source of victory. We can't live the Christian life without studying the Bible. It's the source of truth, it's the source of joy, and it's the source of victory.

Let me give you a fourth one. The Word of God is also:

IV. The Source of Growth

One of the saddest things to see are Christians who don't grow spiritually. The reason they don't grow is because they really don't study the Word. They may go to church, but when they go they take a thimble, fill it up, and spill it on the steps as they're leaving. Nothing ever happens, and that's sad. Peter said in 1 Peter 2:2, "As newborn babes, desire the pure milk of the word, that ye may grow by it." In other words, the Word of God is the source of growth. When I was a younger Christian and in college, I was involved in all sorts of stuff, so I didn't grow much. However, when I got to seminary and got a taste of the Word of God, I found I wanted so much of the Word that I could hardly stand it. I had this tremendous desire to grow, and I realized there was only one way it was going to happen—I had to study the Word of God. My growth, then, was directly proportionate to the amount of time and effort I spent in the study of the Word of God.

But now let's look at some specifics concerning growth.

A. Prerequisites for Growth

1. Sanctification

In 1 Peter 2:1 it is interesting to see how some ground work must first be laid. It says, "laying aside all malice (Gk., *kakia*, 'general evil'), and all guile (which means 'deceit'; the same Greek word is also used for 'fishhook'), and hypocrisies, and envies, and all evil speakings." In other words, we must set aside all evil things, confess our sin, get our life straightened out, and hit the Word with a tremendous desire—then we begin to grow. The more we grow, the more exciting it becomes. The Word is a source of life that helps us mature and grow stronger; then we are able to defeat Satan, and we come to know more about God and His character. We are enriched in every possible way.

2. Study

In John 6:63*b* Jesus says, "The words that I speak unto you, they are spirit, and they are life." Jeremiah said, "Thy words were found, and I did eat them" (15:16a). That's feeding on the Word of God! James 1:18a says, "Of his own will begot he us with the word of truth." The Word is a life-giver, a life-sustainer, and a life-builder. It is tremendous nourishment. First Timothy 4:6 states, "If thou put the brethren in remembrance of these things, thou shalt be a good minister of Jesus Christ, nourished up in the words of faith." Therefore, the Word nourishes us, it feeds us, it builds us, and it causes us to grow.

B. Patterns of Growth (1 John 2:13-14)

God wants us mature; He wants us built up; He wants us strong. In 1 John 2:13 we find the pattern of growth. Listen to what it says: "I write unto you, fathers, because ye have known him that is from the beginning. I write unto you, young men, because ye have overcome the wicked one. I write unto you, little children, because ye have known the Father." There are three categories: fathers, young men, and little children. Now those are three categories of spiritual growth—they are not literally little children, young men, and fathers. It's talking about three levels of *spiritual* growth.

1. Little children

Now we all start out as little children—we know the Father. That's spiritual Da-Da. You don't know much when you're a new Christian, but you know "Jesus loves me, this I know, for the Bible tells me so." You realize God is your Father and it's great, but you're not very mature spiritually. So you don't want to stay there; that would be sad. You go to the second level:

2. Young men

What is the characteristic of a young man? He has overcome the wicked one—past tense. Who is the wicked one? Satan. "Are you telling me that I could reach the point in my life where I actually overcome Satan?" That's right. How? Verse 14 says, "I have written unto you, fathers, because ye have known him that is from the beginning. I have written unto you, young men, because ye are strong, and the word of God abideth in you, and ye have overcome the wicked one." Now listen to this: To overcome Satan you'd have to be strong, and there's only one way to be strong—that's to have the Word abiding in you. Do you know what a spiritual young man is? He's someone who really knows the Word.

Here's why I say that: Satan, according to 2 Corinthians 11:14, comes disguised as an angel of light. I believe Satan spends 99.0 percent of his time in false religious systems. I believe the problems we have with bars, prostitution, crime, the lust of the world, and all the rest of that evil is pretty well taken care of by the flesh. Galatians 5:19-21 lists the works of the flesh. I don't think Satan is running around poking us in the ribs about every little sin; I believe Satan is developing world-wide systems of evil. Satan is appearing as an angel of light, and his ministers are angels of light, and he works in false religions.

Now a spiritual young man is somebody that overcomes Satan in the sense that he knows enough about the Word of God that he is not enticed by false religions. Rather, he is angered by it. For example, the characteristic of a spiritual child, according to Ephesians 4:14, is that he is "tossed to and fro, and carried about with every wind of doctrine." Spiritual babies have trouble with false doctrine. Spiritual young men are people who know their Bible. They know their doctrine, so false doctrine from Satan doesn't appeal to them at all.

But there's a third level:

3. Fathers

In verse 13a John says, "I write unto you, fathers, because ye have known him that is from the beginning." Do you know who the fathers are? They are the ones that have gone beyond the page. They don't just know the doctrine—fathers have a deep knowledge of the God behind the doctrine.

In these three steps we have the progress of spiritual growth. We start out as babies, and as we feed on the Word of God, we become strong. We never totally overcome the flesh, but we can overcome the world; our faith does that (1 John 5:4). The flesh will always be a problem, but we can have the joy of overcoming Satan's false systems of religion. I can tell every time men or women get to the place of being spiritual young people. They invariably get to the place where false religion makes them angry, so they want to go out and fight the cults. Then as they mature, they're not so concerned with fighting the cults—they begin to get a taste of who God is. They begin to plumb the depths of the mind of the eternal God and stretch toward being a spiritual father, walking in the presence of the Holy One. That's where we ought to go in our growth. Listen, you cheat yourself if you stay a baby. You cheat yourself if you stay a spiritual young man and all you know is doctrine. You've got to get to the place where you've begun to walk in the very presence of the God of the universe, where you really begin to touch the Person Himself. That's the ultimate end of growth.

So when you study the Word, it becomes the source of growth. But also, the Word of God is to be studied because it is:

V. The Source of Power

It is the Word of God that infuses us with power, but there's nothing worse than feeling like an impotent Christian. In Acts 1:8a we read, "But ye shall receive power." The Greek word for "power" is *dunamis,* which means "miraculous power" or "dynamite." Now someone might say that you ought to be exploding all over the world with this tremendous power. But you say to yourself, "Exploding! I don't even fizzle. I feel like a dud." Someone else might say that you ought to be out there winning people to Jesus Christ. But you say, "Are you kidding? Not me. I'm like Moses, I—I—I—I can't talk" (cf. Ex. 3:10). Sometimes we get hung up with our impotence because we really don't know the "power" available to us. Listen, the Word of God will infuse us with "power." From my own life I've realized that the more I know about the Word of God, the less I fear any situation, because the Word is my resource. In fact, let's look at various scriptures to see *how* the Bible is a resource for power:

A. Hebrews 4:12—"For the word of God is living, and powerful, and sharper than any two-edged sword, piercing even to the dividing asunder of soul and spirit, and of the joints and marrow, and is a discerner of the thoughts and intents of the heart." When you pick up the Bible and read it, it will cut to the very depths of your being. The Bible is a powerful book!

B. Romans 1:16—The apostle Paul said, "For I am not ashamed of the gospel of Christ; for it is the power of God unto salvation to everyone that believeth." When you share the gospel with someone, you can see its power as it crumbles every bit of false philosophy built up over the years.

C. Ephesians 4:23—"And be renewed in the spirit of your mind." Our thinking will change.

D. Romans 12:2b—"But be ye transformed by the renewing of your mind." There's a life-changing transformation.

E. 2 Corinthians 3:18—"But we all, with unveiled face beholding as in a mirror the glory of the Lord, are changed into the same image from glory to glory, even as by the Spirit of the Lord." As we focus on the Word of God, the power it will have in our lives is incredible. As we meditate on it, it empowers us. It's like the old computer saying, "G.I.G.O., garbage in—garbage out." Whatever we pump into out computers is just what's going to come regurgitating out in our lives. As we feed on the Word of God, it's going to come right back out in our lives. It's our source of energy.

F. Ephesians 1:3–3:20—In the first three chapters of Ephesians the apostle Paul lists several things he wants us to know. They are full of theology and contain some great truths.

First, in chapter 1:

1. Verse 3b—"God . . . who hath blessed us with all spiritual blessings in heavenly places in Christ."

2. Verse 7b—We have "the forgiveness of sins."

3. Verse 7a—"We have redemption."

4. Verse 6b—"He hath made us accepted in the Beloved."

5. Verse 8b—We've been given "all wisdom and prudence."

6. Verses 9-10—We've been given the knowledge of the ages to know the eternal plan of God.

7. Verse 13c—We've been "sealed with that Holy Spirit of promise."

8. Verse 14—We have the Holy Spirit "who is the earnest of our inheritance."

In chapter 2:

9. Verse 22—We are the "habitation of God through the Spirit."

10. Verse 19b—We are "fellow citizens with the saints, and of the household of God."

11. Verse 14b—Christ "hath broken down the middle wall" between Jew and Gentile.

12. Verse 16—We've come together "unto God in one body by the cross."

Then, in chapter 3:

13. Verse 8c—We have "the unsearchable riches of Christ."

14. Verse 9—We have been made to "see what is the fellowship of the mystery, which . . . hath been hidden in God."

All these incredible riches are ours, and Paul wants us to know them. Paul says in 1:17-18 that he prayed that God would "give unto you the spirit of wisdom and revelation in the knowledge of him, the eyes of your understanding being enlightened; that ye may know . . . what (are) the riches of the glory of his inheritance in the saints." So he said if you would learn these truths, then you would realize the truth of what he says in 3:20; "Now unto him who is able to do exceedingly abundantly above all that we ask or think, according to the power that worketh in us." Do you see the resources? Did you ever think about the fact that you can do everything you can think? Did you ever think about the fact that you can do above everything you can think? Did you ever think about the fact that you can do exceedingly, abundantly above all you can ask or think? That's a lot of power, isn't it? Frankly, there's no sense flopping around on one cylinder with those kinds of resources. As you feed on the Word of God it has a powerful effect. It makes your life an energy source that can confront anybody, any time, with the truth.

So we're to study the Word of God because it is the source of truth, the source of happiness, the source of victory, the source of growth, the source of power, and one more: We are to study the Bible because it is:

VI. The Source of Guidance

Whenever I want to know what God wants me to do, I go to the Word. You hear people say, "I'm searching for the will of God." Is God's will lost? They think God is the universal Easter bunny who stashes His will in the bushes and then sits in heaven saying, "You're getting warmer." That isn't true. God's will is easy to find; it's right in His Book. When we study the Bible, we find over and over again the phrase, "This is the will of God." We can know the will of God by studying the Word of God. What does Psalm 119:105 say? "Thy word is a lamp unto my feet, and a light unto my path." That's pretty simple—the Word is a guide. As I open the Word of God, it guides me. It's amazing how God speaks to me through His Word. If I have a decision to make, I find the place in the Bible where possibly someone in the Old Testament or New Testament grappled with a similar decision. I try and see how God led them. Or I'll go to a text in the Bible that gives me a direct answer. God guides and directs us out of His Book.

But there's a subjective element here also: as Christians we have the Holy Spirit (cf. Rom. 8:9). First John 2:27 says, "But the anointing which ye have received of him abideth in you, and ye need not that any man teach you; but as the same anointing teacheth you of all things." When you study the Bible, the Holy Spirit in you takes the Word of God and makes a personal application that will give you guidance. That's an incredible combination—to have the truth and the resident truth teacher. It's that combination that guides the believer. What have we learned? There are great benefits to studying the Bible. It is the source of truth, happiness, victory, growth, power, and guidance.

Conclusion

But what should be our response? If this is really true, if the Bible is going to do all these things, then what shall I do? Let me give you a few things to consider.

1. Believe it

    If the Bible says it—believe it. Jesus said to the twelve one time, "Will ye also go away? Then Simon Peter answered him, Lord, to whom shall we go? Thou hast the words of eternal life" (John 6:67-68). Peter said, "You can't get rid of me. I found the source of truth." If God's Word is true, then hang in there—believe it.

2. Honor it

    If this is the Word of God, then honor it. In Job 23:12*b* there is that magnificent statement of Job when he says, "I have esteemed the words of his mouth more than my necessary food." Listen, if the Bible is the Word of God, and it will do everything we just said it would do, then believe it, and honor it. In fact, in Psalm 138:2*b,* the Psalmist said, "for thou hast magnified thy word above all thy name." Isn't that incredible? God honors the Word.

    In Ephesus, they worshiped the goddess Diana. People think of Diana as some svelte, beautiful thing. But the goddess Diana was an ugly, black beast that was one of the most gross looking things you've ever seen. But they worshiped that stupid looking thing constantly. Do you know why? Because there was a superstition that it fell out of heaven, and if it fell out of heaven it was worthy of honor. Let me tell you something about the Bible—it did come from heaven , but that statue didn't. So believe the Bible and honor it.

3. Love it

    If the Bible is all true, then we had better love it. The psalmist cried out, "Oh, how love I thy law!" (Ps. 119:97). And I love what it says in Psalm 19:10 as it speaks of the statutes of the Lord: "More to be desired are they than gold, yea, than much fine gold; sweeter also than honey and the honeycomb." In fact, verses 7-10 of Psalm 19 compose one of the most beautiful portions of Scripture. So if the Bible said it, believe it, honor it, and love it.

4. Obey it

We commented on this earlier, but if the Bible is true, then we should obey it. Follow the admonition of 1 John 2:5a: "But whosoever keepeth his word, in him verily is the love of God perfected." If it's really what it claims, we should believe it, honor it, love it, and obey it at any price. In fact, it's interesting to see what Romans 6:16a says: "Know ye not that to whom ye yield yourselves servants to obey, his servants ye are whom ye obey." If you yield yourselves as servants to God, you obey Him.

5. Fight for it

I like this one. If it's really true—fight for it! Jude 3 says, "Earnestly contend for the faith." "The faith" means "the body of revealed truth." The Greek word for "earnestly" is *epagonizomai,* from which we get "agonize." Agonize for it; engage yourself in a battle to defend the Word of God. If it's really true, if it can do the things we said it could do, believe it, honor it, love it, obey it, and fight for it.

6. Preach it

In 2 Timothy 4:2a Paul simply said, "Preach the word." If it's really true—preach it. So if we are going to believe it, honor it, love it, obey it, fight for it, and preach it, then we must:

7. Study it

Paul says to Timothy in 2 Timothy 2:15, "Study to show thyself approved unto God, a workman that needeth not to be ashamed, rightly dividing the word of truth." "Rightly dividing" means "cutting it straight." Study it so you can interpret it properly—cut it straight. Paul was using the language of a tentmaker. Now a tentmaker made a tent out of a lot of different animal skins. He had to take every one of those animal skins and cut each piece properly so he could put the whole thing together. If he didn't cut every piece right, then the whole thing wouldn't fit together. In other words, Paul was saying that you can't have theology without exegesis. You can't have the true theology of Christianity unless you have the verses rightly interpreted, cut straight—and that takes study. Spurgeon said every Christian should study the Bible till his blood is Bibline. Do you know what they said about Apollos? In the New Testament they commended him by saying that he was "mighty in the scriptures" (Acts 18:24).

So my prayer for you is that you study the Word of God, that you proclaim it, that you fight for it, that you obey it, that you love it, that you honor it, and that you believe it.

Focusing on the Facts

1. What are the two kinds of obedience? Explain the differences between each one (see p. 24).

2. Why was Peter not supposed to go fishing as he did in John 21:3? What lesson was God teaching him when he couldn't catch any fish (see p. 25)?

3. When Jesus questioned Peter's love for Him, why didn't Peter use the same word that Jesus used when he told him that he did love Him (John 21:15-17; see p. 25)?

4. To what did Peter appeal to prove to Christ that he did love him? Explain (see p. 26).

5. On what basis did Jesus accept Peter's loving commitment to Him (see p. 26)?

6. When does God pour out His blessing and joy on the believer (see p. 27)?

7. What is action fruit without the proper attitude fruit called (see p. 27)?

8. Why is sorrow an important emotion for a believer to experience (see pp. 27-28)?

9. What does the Word of God give Christians victory over? How does it give us victory (see pp. 28-32)?

10. Why did God consider Satan's temptation of Christ a test? Why did Satan consider it a temptation (Matt. 4:1; see p. 29)?

11. What did Satan tempt Jesus to do in Matthew 4:3? How did Jesus respond (Matt. 4:4; see pp. 29-30)?

12. What did Satan tempt Jesus to do in Matthew 4:5-6? How did Jesus respond (Matt. 5:7; see p. 30)?

13. How was Jesus able to command a legion of demons to come out of a man in Luke 4:33-36 (see p. 31)?

14. How is the Word of God like a sword (see pp. 31-32)?

15. What is the only way that Christians will know victory in their lives (see pp. 31-32)?

16. Why don't some Christians grow spiritually (see p. 32)?

17. What are two prerequisites to spiritual growth? Explain each one (see pp. 32-33).

18. What is the pattern of growth that is outlined in 1 John 2:13-14 (see pp. 33-34)?

19. What do believers understand when they are at the first level of spiritual growth (see p. 33)?

20. What is characteristic of the believer at the second level of spiritual growth (see p. 33)?

21. What does Satan spend most of his time doing (2 Cor. 4:4; see p. 34)?

22. What is characteristic of the believer at the third level of spiritual growth (see p. 34)?

23. What are some verses that show how the Bible is a resource for power (see pp. 35-36)?

24. What are some of the riches that God has promised believers (Eph. 1:3—3:12)? What will happen when we learn those truths (see pp. 36-37)?

25. How is the Bible able to guide believers into God's will (see p. 37)?

26. Since the Bible is the source of truth, happiness, victory, growth, power, and guidance, how should Christians respond? Explain each command (see pp. 38-39).

27. According to 2 Timothy 2:15, why do we need to study the Bible (see p. 39)?

Pondering the Principles

1. When God looks into your heart, what does He see? Does He see you obeying Him, but not wanting to obey? Or does He see that you have a sincere willingness to obey Him even when you fail? Are you experiencing happiness in your spiritual walk? If not, you may be obeying God without a true desire. Take this time to examine your heart. Honestly determine why you obey God. Ask Him to reveal your true desires. If there is any aspect of your spiritual walk that is not sincere, confess it to God right now. Ask Him to help you acquire the desire to be obedient to Him in that area of your life.

2. Read Matthew 4:1-11 again. To pass the test that Satan gave Him, on three occasions Jesus quoted a specific portion of Scripture that dealt with Satan's attack. Would you be ready to defend yourself using God's Word if Satan were to attack you? Read 2 Timothy 2:15. You are to be able to handle the Bible accurately. What do you need to do to know it better? Commit yourself to that.

3. Reread the section on the patterns of growth on pages 33-34. What level of growth are you presently at? How do you know? Why aren't you at the next level? What do you have to know better to ascend to

the next level—God's Word or God Himself? What kind of commitment do you have to make to know His Word better? What kind of commitment do you need to make to know God better? Be faithful to maintain that commitment.

4. Review the conclusion on pages 38-40. Do you believe God's Word? How is that manifested in your life? Do you honor God's Word? How do you manifest that? Do you love God's Word? How do you manifest that? Do you obey God's Word at any price? To improve your motivation for obedience, memorize 1 John 2:5. Do you fight for God's Word? How is that manifested in your life? Do you preach or teach God's Word to others? Give some examples of people you have been able to minister to through God's Word. Only as you consistently study God's Word will you find that you will believe, honor, love, obey, fight for, and preach it.

3
Who Can Study the Bible?

Outline

Introduction
A. Know the Word
   1. Hosea 4:1-6
   2. Proverbs 1:20-33
   3. Romans 12:2
   4. Ephesians 4:23
   5. Philippians 1:9
   6. Philippians 4:8*b*
   7. Colossians 1:10*b*
   8. 2 Peter 3:18*a*
   9. 2 Timothy 3:17
  10. Proverbs 24:13-14*a*
B. Live the Word
   1. Luke 11:28
   2. John 14:15
   3. 1 John 5:3*a*
   4. Deuteronomy 5:29
   5. Joshua 1:8
   6. Isaiah 55:9-11
   7. Psalm 138:2
   8. Psalm 119:1-2, 11

Lesson
  I. Those Who Are Believers
   A. Believers Can Understand
   B. Unbelievers Can Not Understand
 II. Those Who Are Diligent
   A. Acts 17:10-12*a*
   B. 2 Timothy 2:15
   C. 1 Timothy 5:17
III. Those Who Have a Great Desire
   A. Hunger for the Word (1 Peter 2:2)
   B. Seek the Word (Job 28:1-18)

Introduction

In the nineteenth century there was a Danish religious philosopher by the name of Søren Kierkegaard. He said many things regarding Christianity and religion that we would not necessarily accept, but every once in a while he would say something rather profound. Let me quote one statement he made: "Too often in their church life people adopt an attitude of the theater, imagining the preacher is an actor and they his critics, praising and blaming the performances. Actually, the people are the actors on the stage of life. The preacher is merely the prompter, reminding the people of their lost lines." I think he perceived a real problem. It's very easy for people to come to church and treat it like a theater, and just sit and watch it happen. Then, they either praise or criticize what went on. But the purpose of a ministry in the pulpit is to stimulate the people in the pew. The reason I study and teach is to stimulate you to study and teach. But the sad part is that there are so many Christians who don't really get into it; they don't study the Bible, so they aren't able to teach it to somebody else.

No doubt there are difficulties and distractions, but that's not a good excuse. I think about Paul when he wrote to Timothy and said, "And the things that thou hast heard from me among many witnesses, the same commit thou to faithful men, who shall be able to teach others also" (2 Tim. 2:2). In other words, "Timothy, what I told you, I want you to tell somebody else."

Paul had to encourage Timothy at this juncture in his life, because Timothy was having many difficulties, and he was beginning to falter. He was having anxiety, and Paul had written him about taking some wine for his stomach's sake (1 Tim. 5:23). People hassled him about his youth, so Paul had said, "Let no man despise thy youth" (1 Tim. 4:12a), and, "Flee also youthful lusts" (1 Tim. 2:22). Timothy was fighting his youth, he was fighting his physical problem, plus, he was basically a timid person. So Paul said, "For God has not given us a spirit of timidity" (2 Tim. 1:7a, NASB).

Timothy was also being attacked by some high-powered religious apostates who had invaded the Ephesian church and were propagating genealogies and a philosophy that he couldn't handle. So Timothy was beginning to falter, but Paul said to him, "You can't stop now, too much is invested in you. Hold to everything that I committed to you, and give it to somebody else." That's the whole point. We can have victory over difficulties, and we need to share God's instruction with others.

Now let's look at some basic facts we need to understand. First, we must:

A. Know the Word

Now if we're going to study the Bible, we've got to be committed to the fact that it needs to be studied. That seems to be basic, so let's look at some passages in Scripture that will help us understand this.

1. Hosea 4:1-6

Hosea was facing the reality in Israel that God's people had abandoned God. Consequently, they fell into all kinds of sin. They became a harlot-wife, an adulterous nation, violating their vow to God. But what was their basic problem? How did it happen? and why did it happen? Well, listen to what he writes beginning in verse 1: "Hear the word of the Lord, ye children of Israel." Stop right there. Hosea puts his finger on the problem. When a nation ceases to hear the Word of the Lord, confusion and chaos take place. He continues, "For the Lord hath a controversy with the inhabitants of the land, because there is no truth, nor mercy, nor knowledge of God in the land." They had removed the foundation, and when the foundation was gone, what was left? Verse 2 gives us the answer, "By swearing, and lying, and killing, and stealing, and committing adultery they break out, and blood toucheth blood." In other words, you get national chaos when you give up the foundation of the Word of God.

In America today people are concerned about the condition of our country; they're concerned about a rising crime problem; they're concerned about the disintegration of the family; they're concerned about chaos in government; they're concerned about economic stress and the chaos that results—the people have all of these concerns in their hearts. But I'll tell you the truth: there is no resolution to any of these problems unless there is a reaffirmation of the absolute qualification of the Word of God as the standard to set the pace for this country.

Israel had failed. When you destroy a biblical base, all you're going to get is chaos. Everything bad had begun to happen because they wouldn't hear the Word of the Lord. Verse 3 says, "Therefore shall the land mourn, and every one that dwelleth in it shall languish, with the beasts of the field, and with the fowls of the heavens; yea, the fish of the sea also shall be taken away." Everything went wrong. Verse 6 sums it up for us: "My people are destroyed." But why? "For lack of knowledge; because thou hast rejected knowledge." Now when a people rejects the law of God and the knowledge of God, they open the floodgates to chaos.

As it is true in a nation, as in the case of Israel, it is also true in the life of an individual. Let's look at a second passage:

2. Proverbs 1:20-33

If you do not have the Word of God as the base of your life, as the orientation for your behavior, as the solid foundation upon which you live—then there is no real base. In Proverbs chapter 1, beginning in verse 20, the writer says, "Wisdom crieth outside; she uttereth her voice in the streets." Then in verse 22: "How long, ye simple ones, will ye love simplicity? And the scoffers delight in their scoffing, and fools hate knowledge." It says they turned a deaf ear and refused to hear (v. 24). Listen, wisdom is available (vv. 23, 25, 33). Give attention to it, or reap the consequences.

What I'm trying to get you to see is how important it is to study the Word of God. It's the foundation of everything. A judge wrote me and asked, "What does the Bible say about what is right in a court of law?" A doctor asked, "What does the Bible say about what is right in terms of how we discipline our children?" Other doctors have written and asked, "What does the Bible say about abortion? What does the Bible say about euthanasia? What does the Bible say about how people are to be treated in certain psychological and psychiatric situations?" The Word of God is the standard! We can't live our lives the way they ought to be lived unless we have the knowledge of God's Word within us. So it's imperative that we be students of His Word.

3. Romans 12:2

"And be not conformed to this world, but be ye transformed." Now how do we get above the system that engulfs us? How do Christians rise above the corruption we live in? How do we ascend beyond the mentality of the day? It says, "Be ye transformed by the renewing of your mind, that ye may prove what is that good, and acceptable, and perfect, will of God." First, you must know the Word before you can live it. If you rush off trying to live life without the knowledge of God's truth, you're going to find yourself right in the middle of the world's system. In order to rise above it, you must know the Word of God.

4. Ephesians 4:23

The apostle Paul says, "And be renewed in the spirit of your mind."

5. Philippians 1:9

Paul says, "I pray, that your love may abound still more and more in real knowledge and all discernment" (NASB).

6. Philippians 4:8b

Paul names a lot of things and then he says, "If there be any virtue, and if there be any praise, *think* on these things."

7. Colossians 1:10b

"Increasing in the knowledge of God."

8. 2 Peter 3:18a

"But grow in grace, and in the knowledge of our Lord and Savior, Jesus Christ."

9. 2 Timothy 3:17

The Word of God is provided so "that the man of God may be perfect, thoroughly furnished unto all good works."

10. Proverbs 24:13-14a

This is a beautiful statement about knowledge: "My son, eat thou honey, because it is good, and the honeycomb, which is sweet to thy taste; so shall the knowledge of wisdom be unto thy soul." In fact, all through the thirty-one chapters of Proverbs is the injunction to learn God's truth, to know it, to live it—and over and over again it tells us to seek wisdom. By the way, every Hebrew boy, as he grew up, was taught the book of Proverbs so he might know God's standard for life.

As we come to know the Word, we must also:

B. Live the Word

The knowledge of which Scripture speaks is not separated from obedience. Scripture knows nothing of theories. It knows nothing of the intellectualism of the Greek "wisdom," *sophia* (theoretical knowledge). The Hebrew thought of wisdom was always in the context of "behavior." In fact, to the Hebrew, if you didn't live it, you didn't really know it. To the Greek, wisdom (*sophos*) was intellectualizing, it was theory, it was conceptual. But to the Hebrew, wisdom was life, it was living, it was behaving in a manner in accord with the law of God. *Wisdom wasn't just conceiving, wisdom was walking.*

So where the Bible draws us to knowledge, and where it draws us to wisdom, and to understanding, and to enlightenment, and to perception—it is always with a view of behavior. You never really know it until you live it.

But let's look at Scripture to expand our understanding of this vital principle:

1. Luke 11:28

   "Blessed are they that hear the word of God, and *keep* it."

2. John 14:15

   Jesus said, "If ye love me, *keep* my commandments."

3. 1 John 5:3*a*

   "For this is the love of God, that we *keep* his commandments."

4. Deuteronomy 5:29

   "Oh, that there were such an heart in them, that they would fear me, and *keep* all my commandments always, that it might be well with them and with their children forever!"

5. Joshua 1:8

   The Lord told Joshua that he was required to study and reflect on the Word of God. He said, "This book of the law shall not depart out of thy mouth, but thou shalt meditate therein day and night, that thou mayest *observe to do* according to all that is written therein; for then thou shalt make thy way prosperous, and then thou shalt have good success." In other words, "Joshua, you must be committed to the law of God."

   Chaos existed in Israel when the law was lost. Finally, when it was found, they stood up and read it. A revival broke out because they had again found the standard for life (2 Chron. 34:14-32).

6. Isaiah 55:9-11

   "For as the heavens are higher than the earth, so are my ways higher than your ways, and my thoughts than your thoughts. For as the rain cometh down, and the snow from heaven, and returneth not there, but watereth the earth, and maketh it bring forth and bud, that it may give seed to the sower, and bread to the eater, so shall my word be that goeth

48

forth out of my mouth; it shall not return unto me void, but it shall accomplish that which I please, and it shall prosper in the thing whereto I sent it." God said, "As the rain and snow comes down and waters the earth, so My Word will come down and give growth to your life."

7. Psalm 138:2

David was a man with a worshiping heart, and he worshiped God with these words: "I will worship toward thy holy temple, and praise thy name for thy loving-kindness and for thy truth; for thou hast magnified thy word above all thy name." David said, "God, I will worship You on the basis of Your truth." *We can't truly worship God, no matter how meaningful that might be in our own mind, unless we worship Him according to truth.* In John 4:24 Jesus says, "they that worship him must worship him in spirit and in truth." You can't devise your own means for worship. Like Saul, you can't offer the Lord a whole lot of animals that you stole against His commandment and then say, "Well, I'm serving the Lord" (cf. 1 Sam. 13:10-14). God doesn't want self-styled worship, He wants it according to His Word. *True worship is lived out in the lives of believers who love His Word.*

8. Psalm 119:1-2, 11

Psalm 119 is one of the most majestic poems in all of holy writ. Nearly every one of the 176 verses teaches us the necessity of obedience to the Word of God. It begins by saying, "Blessed are the undefiled in the way, who walk in the law of the Lord. Blessed are they that *keep* his testimonies, and that seek him with the whole heart." Then in verse 11, "Thy word have I hidden in mine heart that I might not sin against thee."

So we find that the Scripture calls us to obey the Word. Scripture after scripture after scripture tells us of the importance of the Word.

Would you make a covenant with me?

Can I ask you to make a covenant in your heart? I don't want to impose it on you, I just want you to do it because it's right. You may say, "Well, this Bible study is hard work." Yes, but these things were written "that your joy might be full" (John 15:11*b*). Do you want full joy in your life? That's why God wrote the Bible. Would you make a covenant? And I'll give you a covenant so you don't have to think up your own. This covenant was made by Josiah the king, and God really blessed him for it. In 2 Chronicles 34:31 it says, "And the king stood in his place, and made a covenant before the Lord." This young man Josiah was like a beam of light in the midst of the darkness of ancient Israel. He was a godly man and he made a covenant before the Lord. Now listen to it: "to walk after the Lord, and to *keep* his commandments, and his testimonies, and his statutes, with all his heart, and with all his soul, *to perform the words of the covenant which are written in this book*" (emphasis added). Josiah said, "Lord, as long as I live, this day I vow to learn and to live Your Word." That's why he was different than everybody before him and after him. We can rise above the crowd too if we make that same covenant with the Lord. Are you willing to make that covenant?

Now who can actually study the Bible? I've said that everybody *should* study it, but who *can* study it and get something out of it? You might say, "Well, I'll have to go to seminary," or, "I'll have to get a lot of books to understand it." Will you? Now there are a lot of people who purport to understand the Bible, and they knock on your door and tell you that they'll explain it to you. But who can really understand the Bible? What are the basic requirements? Well, let me give you six requirements for who is able to understand the Bible.

Lesson

I. Those Who Are Believers

A. Believers *Can* Understand

To understand the Bible, a person must be a true Christian, a believer, born again, regenerated. "You mean if you're not a Christian you can't understand the Bible?" That's right! In 1 Corinthians 2, beginning in verse 10, we find a tremendous insight. It says, "But God hath revealed them unto us by his Spirit." Now the word "them" refers to God's truths, God's principles, or God's Word. But *who* receives them? Notice the little phrase "unto us." Now that might not seem too important in the English, but it is important in the Greek because "unto us" comes at the beginning of the sentence, and it is in the emphatic form. Paul is saying that the revelation of God's truth is "unto us," and the "us" refers to believers. This is in contrast to the ones he has previously been referring to. From chapter 1, verse 18, to chapter 2, verse 9, he is talking about how ignorant the philosophers of the world are in regard to the truth of God.

But why can't they know the truth of God? Because it says in verse 9 of chapter 2, "Eye hath not seen." They can't see it empirically—they can't find it out by discovery. Then, "neither have entered into the heart of man." They can't find it by their own feeling, or by their own emotion, or by their own musings, or by their own spiritual experience. God's truth is not available externally, and it is not available internally, no matter how erudite the philosopher may be. Why? Because God has revealed it "unto us," not to them. Paul says in verse 6 that there are those in the world who speak human wisdom—"the princes of this age"—but none of these princes knew the truth (v. 8). It's not available to them. Why? Because in their humanness they *can't* know it. Verse 11 says, "For what man knoweth the things of a man, except the spirit of man which is in him? Even so the things of God knoweth no man, but the Spirit of God." If a man does not have the indwelling Spirit, he can't know the truth of God. Now he may think he knows some things, and he may try to figure some things out, but he can't truly know—at least not in the sense of knowing and living out that truth in life. But concerning Christians, verse 12 says, "Now we have received, not the spirit of the world." The "spirit of the world" is a paraphrase for human reason. Christians don't depend on human reason, we depend on "the Spirit who is of God." And because of Him we "know the things that are freely given to us of God."

B. Unbelievers *Cannot* Understand

The essence of the unbeliever is summed up in verse 14 of 1 Corinthians 2: "But the natural man receiveth not the things of the Spirit of God; for they are foolishness unto him, neither can he know them, because they are spiritually discerned." If you're not a believer, you cannot really perceive with understanding the truth of God. It is the same analogy of verse 11: A man cannot know anything about himself unless he knows it in his spirit. Listen, a dead body doesn't know anything because it has no spirit. Likewise, a man without the Spirit of God is like a physically dead body because he can't know anything spiritually. One prime aspect of spiritual death is the absence of the knowledge of God, because of the absence of the Spirit of God.

So, without knowing Christ you can't know the Bible. That's what's so sad about the cults; they concoct elaborate theology, but they don't even know God to begin with, and they deny Jesus Christ. Therefore, confusion is just added upon confusion, and the truth becomes hopelessly muddled. The truth is only available to those who know and love the Lord Jesus Christ. Martin Luther said, "Man is like a pillar of salt, he's like Lot's wife, he's like a log or a stone, he's like a lifeless statue which uses neither eyes nor mouth, neither sense nor heart until that man is converted and regenerated by the Holy Spirit. And until that happens, man will never know God's truth." So the bottom line on knowing the Bible is that you know God through Jesus Christ; the believing heart will understand God's Word.

Our Lord makes a profound comment in John 8:44 when He says to the Pharisees, "Ye are of your father the devil. . . . for he is a liar, and the father of it." Then He says in verse 45, "And because I tell you the truth, ye believe me not." Amazing! The reason they didn't believe Him was because He told them the truth, and that was something they couldn't perceive. Now that is the state of unregenerate man and the condition of unbelievers. If you tell them the truth, they don't receive it because they can't perceive it.

However, I believe there is a point at which an unbeliever will become open to God, when with a searching heart he says, "Lord, teach me Your truth, I want to know if Christ is real." If there's an open heart, there's a transition time when the truth is brought to you and you're regenerated. In general, the natural man will never know the truth when he reasons from his own mind. Only when he opens his heart to be instructed by God and he begins to seek Christ will the truth become evident. Then once he's converted, the Spirit will be within him to teach him the truth.

A second requirement for who can study the Bible is:

II. Those Who Are Diligent

In order to study the Bible we must be diligent. We can't study Scripture in a haphazard way—there's got to be a commitment to it. Let's take a look at some scriptures to see what I mean:

A. Acts 17:10-12a

In Acts chapter 17 the apostle Paul was moving around in his ministry to the Gentiles. He had been in Thessalonica, and he proceeded from there south to Berea. Beginning in verse 10: "And the brethren immediately sent away Paul and Silas by night unto Berea, who, coming there, went into the synagogue of the Jews. These were more noble than those in Thessalonica, in that they received the word with all readiness of mind." Now this was great! Here were some open minds that were ready to receive the

Word, "and searched the scriptures daily, whether those things were so. Therefore, many of them believed." They were more noble than the rest because they were diligent in their study of the Scriptures. I believe they were true Old Testament saints who knew God under the terms of the Old Testament. Their hearts were cracked wide open when the gospel came in because they were open to receive it and they searched diligently. By the way, the word for "search" is a judicial term meaning "an investigation." They really got into it and investigated it to see if it was true. You can't study the Bible in a haphazard manner.

B. 2 Timothy 2:15

In this verse it says, "Be diligent" (NASB). Paul used a tremendously strong word: "Be diligent (NASB) to show thyself approved unto God, a workman that needeth not to be ashamed, rightly dividing the word of truth" (KJV*). You need to be diligent in your Bible study. Why? So you can rightly divide it. If you don't, you'll have something to be ashamed of, and you will not be approved. Oh, that word "approved" is a great word. In the Greek it is *dokimos,* which means, "proven, tested, shown to be of high quality." A high-quality Christian, an approved Christian, one who has no flaws for which he will be ashamed—he is the one who is diligent to study the Word of God.

The words "rightly dividing" mean literally "to cut it straight." Paul made tents; he used these words because he made tents out of goatskins, and he had to cut the hides properly so they would fit together. Paul said you have "to cut straight" every portion of Scripture or the whole doesn't come together. You can't make sense out of the whole unless you know what to do with the parts. You must cut every portion of the Word of God straight and then fit the whole together.

C. 1 Timothy 5:17

"Let the elders that rule well be counted worthy of double honor, especially they who labor (work hard) in the word and doctrine." Paul used *kopiaō,* which is a Greek verb that means "to work to the point of sweat and exhaustion." There has to be a commitment to diligence and hard work when you search the Scriptures.

So, if you're going to be a Bible student, if you're going to make a personal commitment to learn the Scriptures: First, you must know Jesus Christ as your Savior so you have the Spirit to teach you. Second, you must be diligent. Third, and maybe this should be the apex

---

* *King James Version.*

of our thoughts, the ones *who* will understand the Bible are:

III. Those Who Have a Great Desire

Becoming a good Bible student will not happen by accident. You've got to want it. Let's look at various Scriptures that illustrate this necessity:

A. Hunger for the Word (1 Pet. 2:2)

"As newborn babes, desire the pure milk of the word, that ye may grow by it." A baby desires one thing—milk! It doesn't care about anything else. It doesn't care what the color of the curtains or the carpet is, it doesn't care what the color of the booties or nightgown it's wearing may be, it doesn't care what car you buy—a baby wants milk. A baby has singlemindedness, and Peter said, "Like a baby desires milk, and only milk, so should our hunger be for the Word."

B. Seek the Word (Job 28:1-18)

I love what it says in Proverbs 2:4 regarding knowledge and understanding: "Seekest her as silver." Can you imagine how hard people work to find silver? That's the way we ought to seek the knowledge of God's Word. I think Job has the most marvelous speech on this subject in the twenty-eighth chapter of Job. He gave a tremendous speech on mining, and then he applied it to the Word. Beginning in verse 1: "Surely there is a vein for the silver, and a place for gold where they refine it. Iron is taken out of the earth, and bronze is smelted out of the stone." He said that men go to all lengths in mining. "He setteth an end to darkness, and searcheth out all perfection, the stones of darkness, and the shadow of death" (v. 3). He said they burrow into the earth like a bunch of moles, into pitch-black darkness, and they get themselves surrounded by very dangerous situations. They'll do anything to find what they're looking for. "The flood breaketh out from the inhabitant; even the waters forgotten by the foot; they are dried up, they are gone away from men" (v. 4). The idea here is that of changing the configuration of the earth by mining and digging it all out. Verse 9 says they literally overturn the mountains by the roots. In verse 7 they go where no bird has ever been, and in verse 8: "The lion's whelps have not trodden it, nor the fierce lion passed by it." They cut rivers among the rocks, and they dam up other places in verse 11. All this digging, to find precious metal.

In our society, we dig and hunt and go to tremendous extremes to buy gold and silver to hang on our fingers, arms, necks, and ears.

54

And just think of the tremendous expense involved. We mine for precious metals, and we go to great lengths to do so; yet, with all the advancement, and all the technology, and all the luxury, gold, and silver, the one thing we don't have is wisdom. Job points this out very clearly in verse 12: "But where shall wisdom be found? And where is the place of understanding?" Where can we mine understanding?

"The depth saith, It is not in me; and the sea saith, It is not with me. It cannot be gotten for gold, neither shall silver be weighed for the price of it. It cannot be valued with the gold of Ophir, with the precious onyx, or the sapphire. The gold and the crystal cannot equal it; and the exchange of it shall not be for jewels of fine gold. No mention shall be made of coral, or of pearls; for the price of wisdom is above rubies" (vv. 14-18). In other words, Job said that in man's earth, and in man's economy, wisdom is not found. The implication is that man is a fool to spend such energy to find metal and then spend none to find truth. God help us to seek the wisdom in His Word as much as men seek precious metal from the earth.

C. Treasure the Word (Job 23:12b)

Do you have a desire for His Word? Do you have an overwhelming passion for His Word? Here's a great verse: "I have treasured the words of His mouth more than my necessary food" (NASB). If it came down to working for my food or studying the Bible, it would be His Word. If it came down to eating food or feeding on the Word, it would be His Word; for I treasure that above everything else. That's the kind of hunger the Psalmist must have been referring to when he said: "Oh, how I love Thy law!" (Ps. 119:97, NASB). He says in Psalm 19:10b that the truth was "sweeter also than honey and the honeycomb." So, we must have a great desire for God's Word.

Well, what if you don't have that desire? How then do you get it? Even if you don't seem to have the desire, all these requirements will come together. If you're born again, that's only the first requirement. If you're born again and diligent, that's just the first two. If you're born again, diligent, and you have a great desire, that's just three—but there's more. And if you're weak in one, it will be strengthened by another. Now what is the fourth requirement for who can study the Bible?

IV. Those Who Are Holy

In order to study the Word of God, there must be holiness. Well, where do you get that? Let's look at just two verses:

55

A. 1 Peter 2:1

"**Wherefore**, laying aside all malice [Gk., *kakia,* 'general evil'], and all guile [deceit] and hypocrisies, and envies, and all evil speakings—" In other words, clean up your act, maintain holiness, pursue righteousness, get your life pure, and then "—desire the pure milk of the word, that ye may grow by it" (v. 2.). If the desire isn't there, then you had better back up to verse 1. Do you see why I said you have to take them all together? If you're born again, and if you're holy and righteous (i.e., dealing with sin in your life by confessing it), out of that born-again reality and the holiness of your life will grow the diligent desire to study.

B. James 1:21

It says at the end of the verse, "receive with meekness the engrafted word." Receive with humility the Word. That's a great thought, but you can't do that unless you go to the first part of the verse: "Wherefore, put away all filthiness and overflowing of wickedness, and receive with meekness the engrafted word." The Word cannot do its work in a sinful life because it is not a conceptual thing, it is a living reality. It isn't just thought, it's life.

So what is the Word of God saying to us? Who can study the Bible? Someone who is born again; someone who is willing to be diligent and search the Scripture; someone who has a strong and hungering desire for it—a desire that is born out of holiness and righteousness; and fifth, in order to study the Word of God effectively, it is limited to:

V. Those Who Are Spirit-Controlled

How wonderful it is to study the Scripture and know that I not only have the page in my hand, but I have the Author in my heart. The Author is the Spirit of God who is the teacher. First John 2:20 says, "But ye have an unction from the Holy One, and ye know all things." Now just stated by itself that verse may not make a lot of sense, but let me give you the context: John was talking about false teachers—antichrists. The Gnostics, who were a group of people who thought they knew everything (Gk., *gnōsis,* "to know"), said, "We know because we have an anointing." They thought they had a special anointing that elevated them above everybody else. But John said to the Christians, "You're the ones with the unction; you're the ones with the anointing. You don't have some mystical Gnostic anointing; you have an anointing from the Holy One, and you know all things." In verse 27 he elucidates further on the same thought: "But the anointing which ye have received of him abideth in you." What is this anointing that lives in us? It's the Spirit of God. And since the Spirit of God lives within us, we don't need human teachers because *He* teaches us. John said that we don't need teachers to teach us human wisdom. Why? Because we have an anointing—the Spirit of God.

It's obvious then that we need to be born again, be diligent, have a strong desire, live a holy life, and be Spirit-filled—Spirit-controlled because the Spirit is the One who teaches and applies the Word to our lives. But there's one other thing: all this has to come together in an atmosphere of prayer. So the sixth requirement for who can study the Bible is:

VI. Those Who Are Prayerful

You could draw a circle around the other five requirements and encompass them with prayer. I believe our Bible study must be born out of prayer. When I study the Bible I pray this simple prayer: "Lord, as I approach your Word, show me Your truth and teach me what I must know." I would never approach the Scripture without first seeking God in prayer.

Paul, in Ephesians 1:15-18*a,* says, "I . . . cease not to give thanks for you, making mention of you in my prayers: that the God of our Lord Jesus Christ, the Father of glory, may give unto you the spirit of wisdom and revelation in the knowledge of him, the eyes of your understanding being enlightened; that ye may know." Paul says, "I'm praying for you." What are you praying for, Paul? "That you'll know, that your eyes will be open, that you'll understand, and that you'll see the truth." If Paul prayed for us to understand God's Word, then we are well instructed to pray as he did.

Who can study the Bible? Listen, you've got to be the right *who* or the *how* won't matter. Are you born again? Do you have a strong desire in your heart? Are you diligent? Holy? Spirit-controlled? Prayerful? If you are, then you can open the pages of the Bible, and God will reveal His truths to your heart. When your life is right, then the method of how to study the Bible will become productive and life-changing as you study His Word.

Focusing on the Facts

1. What is the purpose of the preacher's ministry from the pulpit (see p. 44)?

2. What were some of the problems that Timothy faced in his ministry? What did Paul encourage him to do (2 Tim. 2:2; see p. 44)?

3. What happens when a nation ceases to hear God's Word (Hos. 4:1-2; see p. 45)?

4. What kind of foundation does a person have if he doesn't have God's Word as his base (see pp. 45-46)?

5. How can a Christian rise above the corruption of the world system (Rom. 12:2; see pp. 46-47)?

6. What injunction is scattered throughout the thirty-one chapters of Proverbs (see p. 47)?

7. Describe the differences between the Greek and Hebrew concepts of *wisdom*. Which concept does the Bible follow (see p. 47)?

8. What is the only way that we can truly worship God (John 4:24)? How is that manifested (see p. 49)?

9. What is the main thing that Psalm 119 teaches (see p. 49)?

10. What was the covenant that Josiah made in 2 Chronicles 34:31 (see p. 50)?

11. Who are the only people who can understand the Bible? Why can't anyone else understand it (1 Cor. 2:9-14; see pp. 50-51)?

12. How is a man without the Spirit of God like a dead body (see p. 51)?

13. What was the response of the Pharisees when Jesus told them the truth (John 8:45; see p. 52)?

14. What is the only way that a natural man can ever begin to know God's truth (see p. 52)?

15. Why were the people in Berea more noble than those in Thessalonica (Acts 17:10-11; see pp. 52-53)?

16. The Bereans *searched* the Scriptures (Acts 17:11). What does that mean (see p. 53)?

17. Why do we need to be diligent in our study of the Bible? Explain (2 Tim. 2:15; see p. 53)?

18. How hard should you work at your Bible study (1 Tim. 5:17; see p. 53)?

19. What should Christians be like in their hunger for God's Word (1 Pet. 2:2; see p. 54)?

20. What does Proverbs 2:4 say about how we should seek knowledge and understanding (see p. 54)?

21. To study the Bible a person must be holy, but how does he become holy? How will that help his desire to study God's Word (1 Pet. 2:1-2; see p. 56)?

22. Who teaches us when we study the Bible (1 John 2:20, 27; see pp. 56-57)?

23. What is the first thing a believer should do before he starts to study

God's Word (Eph. 1:15-18; see p. 57)?

Pondering the Principles

1. The Hebrews associated wisdom with behavior, while the Greeks conceived of it as an intellectual exercise. When you learn some spiritual truth, are you like a Hebrew or a Greek? Do you put that truth into action, or do you merely meditate on it as good instruction without applying it? What spiritual truths are you very familiar with that you have yet to put into practice? Be honest in your analysis. Make a list of those truths. Next to each one, indicate how you plan to put it into practice in the next week. Once you have started, be committed to faithfully practicing them until they become part of you.

2. In 2 Chronicles 34:31 Josiah made a covenant "to walk after the Lord, and to keep His commandments and His testimonies and His statutes with all his heart and with all his soul, to perform the words of the covenant written in this book" (NASB). Are you willing to make that same covenant with God? Begin that covenant by first memorizing 2 Chronicles 34:31.

3. Many Christians honestly have trouble with their desire to study God's Word, but here is a way to increase that desire: Pursue holiness. Look up the following verses: 2 Corinthians 7:1; Ephesians 4:21-24; 2 Timothy 2:21-22; 1 Peter 1:14-16; 2 Peter 1:5-8. What do those verses teach you about holiness? According to 2 Peter 1:5, what do you need to add to virtue (or moral excellence)? What is the only way to obtain that? But what must you first add virtue to? Be faithful to be holy in all your behavior, and your desire to study God's Word will increase.

4. The most important thing to do before you study the Bible is to pray. It also should be the last thing you do. Right now, thank God for the things He has taught you through this particular study. Ask Him to help you apply the truths He has taught you. The next time you get ready to study the Bible, be sure to ask God to teach you those truths that will be most applicable to your spiritual walk. Thank Him right now for the treasure that His Word is in your life.

4
How to Study the Bible

Outline

Introduction

Lesson
I. Read the Bible
 A. The Old Testament
 B. The New Testament
  1. The method
  2. The merit
II. Interpret the Bible
 A. Errors of Interpretation
  1. Don't make a point at the price of proper interpretation
   a) The Tower of Babel
   b) Salvation lost
  2. Avoid superficial interpretation
  3. Don't spiritualize
 B. Sources of Interpretation
  1. The language
  2. The culture
  3. The geography
  4. The history
 C. Principles of Interpretation
  1. The literal principle
  2. The historical principle
  3. The grammatical principle
  4. The synthesis principle
  5. The practical principle
III. Meditate on the Bible
IV. Teach the Bible

Introduction

I don't know if you've ever really thought about the magnificence of the Bible and what a privilege we have in studying it, but I hope because of this study you'll be able to focus in on some of the tremendous things that await you in the Scripture as you break it open.

An architect's view of the Bible

Some time ago I read an illustration that went something like this: The Bible is like a magnificent palace constructed of precious Oriental stone, comprising sixty-six stately chambers. Each one of these rooms is different from its fellows and is perfect in its individual beauty; yet, when viewed as a whole, they form an edifice—incomparable, majestic, glorious, and sublime. In the book of Genesis, we enter the vestibule, where we are immediately introduced to the records of the mighty works of God in creation. This vestibule gives access to the law courts, the passage way to the picture gallery of the historical books. Here we find hung on the walls scenes of battles, heroic deeds, and portraits of valiant men of God. Beyond the picture gallery we find the philosopher's chamber (the book of Job), passing through which we enter the music room (the book of Psalms). Here we linger, thrilled by the grandest harmonies that ever fell on human ears. And then we come to the business office (the book of Proverbs), in the very center of which stands the motto: "Righteousness exalteth a nation, but sin is a reproach to any people" (14:34). Leaving the business office, we pass into the research department—Ecclesiastes. From there we proceed into the conservatory (the Song of Solomon), where the fragment aroma of choicest fruits and flowers and the sweetest singing of birds greet us. Then, we reach the observatory where the prophets with their powerful telescopes are looking for the appearing of the Bright and Morning Star prior to the dawning of the Son of righteousness. Crossing the courtyard, we come to the audience chamber of the King (the gospels), where we find four lifelike portraits of the King Himself that reveal the perfections of His infinite beauty. Next, we enter the workroom of the Holy Spirit (the book of Acts) and, beyond, the correspondence room (the epistles), where we see Paul, Peter, James, John, and Jude busy at their tables under the personal direction of the Spirit of Truth. And finally, we enter the throne room (the book of Revelation), where we are enraptured by the mighty volume of adoration and praise addressed to the enthroned King, which fills the vast chamber; while, in the adjacent galleries and judgment hall, there are portrayed solemn scenes of doom and wonderous scenes of glory associated with the coming manifestation of the King of kings and Lord of lords.

> Oh, the majesty of this Book, from creation to the culmination.
> How it behooves us to be diligent in our study!

But *how* do we go about it? How can we really understand the Bible?

Lesson

I. Read the Bible

Bible study begins with reading it. But quite frankly, a lot of people never get to that point. They sort of nibble at it, but they never really read it. They may read a lot of books about it, but they don't really read the Bible, and there is no substitute for reading the Scripture. We must be totally committed to reading it because that's where it all begins. My suggestion is that you try to read through the Bible once a year.

First, let's discuss how we should read:

A. The Old Testament

I believe Christians should try to read through the Old Testament once a year. There are thirty-nine books in the Old Testament, and if you read about twenty minutes a day, you should be able to get through it in one year.

Now the Old Testament is written in the Hebrew language, which is a very simple language. It doesn't have the lofty concepts of the Greek thinking; it isn't a theoretical language, it isn't a conceptual language, and it isn't a philosophical language with a lot of abstraction. It's a very simple, very concrete language. In fact, as a student in seminary, I found the study of Hebrew infinitely easier than the study of Greek. It is just not a complex language. So you can read through the narrative of the Old Testament, for the most part, year after year, and all the while build a comprehension as you read. I would also suggest that as you read the Bible, mark in the margin a notation where you don't understand what it's talking about. If you do that, you'll find an interesting thing will happen. As time goes on you will begin to check them off your margin, because as you read and reread the Scripture from Genesis to Malachi, an understanding will become yours that will answer some of those questions you had. The ones you don't answer in your reading, you can use for individual study with a commentary or other source to find the meaning. But begin by just reading it. Don't become overwhelmed and think, "How can I ever learn the meaning of every verse? Just begin to read through the Old Testament at least once a year.

B. The New Testament

Now I have a little different plan for reading the New Testament. And by the way, I think our major thrust should be reading the New Testament. I believe that's scriptural. In Colossians 1:25-26 Paul said, "Of which I am made a minister, according to the dispensation of God which is given to me for you, to fulfill the word of God, even the mystery which hath been hidden from ages and from generations, but now is made manifest to his saints." Paul said, "I'm called by God to give you the mystery that's been hidden." Now the mystery, basically, is the New Testament revelation. Paul also said that he was an apostle of the "mystery" in Ephesians 3:3-5. So the major thrust of his ministry was the new revelation. He would allude to the Old Testament insofar as it illustrated and elucidated and supported the New Testament.

So the message of the New Testament is the culmination of revelation. It is that which embodies and engulfs all that was in the Old Testament. In a sense, the New Testament will summarize for you the content of the Old Testament, as well as lead you further into the fullness of revelation. So when you read the New Testament you must spend more time in it because it explains the Old Testament. Also, it is written in the Greek language, which is a more complex, perhaps more difficult language to understand than the Hebrew because it talks more in abstractions and concepts, rather than narrative stories. For this reason we need a greater diligence in studying the New Testament.

Now here's how I've done it:

1. The method

When I was in seminary I decided to read 1 John every day for thirty days. You can do it this way too. The first day just read 1 John all the way through. It will only take you twenty-five or thirty minutes. The idea is to read it through the first day, then on the second day read it through again; on the third day, read it through again; on the fourth day, read it through again; on the fifth day, read it through again. Just sit down and read it. Now about the seventh or eighth day you're going to say to yourself, "This is getting old. Besides, I've got this stuff pretty well under my belt." But that's the tough part. If you push through and just stick with it for thirty days, you'll have a tremendous comprehension of 1 John.

Basically, this is what I do all the time. As I prepare messages, I just read through the book over and over again until the whole book fills my mind in a kind of visual perception. I would also suggest that you take a three by five card and write down the major theme of each chapter. Then, every day when you read the book, just look at the card and read through the list. What will happen is you'll begin to learn what's in the chapters.

Now when you've finished reading 1 John for thirty days, where do you go next? I suggest that you go to a large book in the New Testament. (And remember, all the time you're still reading the narrative of the Old Testament twenty minutes a day.) I believe you should go from 1 John to the gospel of John. "But that's twenty-one chapters!" That's right, so just divide it into three sections. Read the first seven for thirty days, the second seven for thirty days, and the third seven for thirty days. At the end of those ninety days you will have pretty well mastered the content of the gospel of John. And by the way, you've also had a three by five card on the first seven chapters, one on the second seven, and one of the third seven. So you've memorized the major theme of each chapter.

But what does this method of Bible study really accomplish?

2. The merit

I remember when I started using this method it was really amazing how fast I began to retain the things in the New Testament. I had always wanted to make sure that I didn't wind up a concordance cripple, never being able to find anything in the Bible and having to look up the verses in the back. And to this day, the gospel of John, 1 John, and the other books of the New Testament have stuck in my mind. Why? Because this is how we learn. Isaiah said you learn line upon line, line upon line, precept on precept, precept on precept, here a little, and there a little (cf. Isa. 28:10, 13). When you study for a test, you don't pick up your book, read through the notes once, and say, "I've got it." At least, not if you're normal. You learn by repetition, repetition, repetition. That's the way to learn the Bible.

After the gospel of John you might want to go to Philippians, another short book. Then you might want to go to Matthew, and then to Colossians, then to Acts. Divide it up like that, back and forth, a small book and a large book. "But that's going to take a long time!" No. In approximately two-and-one-half years you will have finished the whole New Testament! That's great! You're going to read the Bible anyway, so you might as well read it so you can remember it. Some people may say, "Well, I have my devotions, and I read a passage for the day." That's fine. But you might say, "What was it?" They may say, "Umm, let's see, umm." Or, "What was it three days ago?" "Umm—" It just may be next to hopeless. It's really difficult to retain anything by moving fast. You must go over it and over it and over it. If you believe the Bible is the living Word, it will come alive in your life as you read it in a repetitious manner.

Should I always read from the same version?

Generally, yes. Stay with the same version so you will have familiarity. Once in a while it's good to read the passage from another version just to further elucidate it. I normally read in the King James Version, but just for my own edification I'll invariably read the passage I'm studying in the *New American Standard Version* or the *New International Version*. I think those two are the best available comparative translations.

Reading the Bible answers this question: What does the Bible say? We have to read it to find out exactly what it says. Let me tell you another interesting thing that happens when you begin to read the Bible repetitiously: you will find that your total comprehension will increase incredibly. That's because the Bible explains the Bible. And just as a footnote, there's an excellent book that will help you see how one part of the Bible will explain another part of the Bible. The book is called *The Treasury of Scripture Knowledge,* by R. A. Torrey (Revell, 1973). It goes through all the verses of the Bible and gives you cross reference verses that help explain the meaning of a particular text. So, when you begin to read the Bible, you're going to find a lot of the gaps being filled in because you can understand it. After all, God did not write a book to trip you up. The Bible is not a book that's supposed to have some kind of hidden truth—it's not a secret book. You're *supposed* to discover what God is trying to say. But some people will say, "Whatever you do, don't read the book of Revelation; it's so confusing." But it says in chapter 1, verse 3*a*, "Blessed is he that readeth, and they that hear the words of this prophecy." It's not that tough. But I'll tell you one thing, you'll never fully understand Revelation unless you're reading through Daniel and Isaiah and Ezekiel. It all begins to come together when you read the whole Word of God. You will be amazed at what will take place in your life.

So, the first principle on *how* to study the Bible is to *read it*. The second one is:

II. Interpret the Bible

There are some people who don't interpret the Bible, they just apply it. They read it and go directly to applying it without ever interpreting it. They simply don't bother to find out what it really means. Our first point was to *read* the Bible. That will answer the question: What does the Bible say? The second point, *interpret* the Bible, answers the question: What does the Bible mean by what it says? We have to interpret the Bible. We can't just say, "Well, I had my devotions, and I was reading along, and I just decided this is what it means." No. You have to *know* what it means.

In chapter 8 of Nehemiah we have an interesting passage, beginning in verse 1: "And all the people gathered themselves together as one man into the street that was before the water gate; and they spoke unto Ezra, the scribe, to bring the book of the law of Moses, which the Lord had commanded to Israel. And Ezra, the priest, brought the law before the congregation both of men and women, and all who could hear with understanding, upon the first day of the seventh month. And he read from it facing the street that was before the water gate from the morning until midday" (vv. 1-3*a*). Now this is where it all begins, you have to read the Bible. Continuing in verse 3*c*: "And the ears of all the people were attentive unto the book of the law." Then in verse 5-6: "And Ezra opened the book in the sight of all the people (for he was above all the people); and when he opened it, all the people stood up. And Ezra blessed the Lord, the great God. And all the people answered, Amen, Amen, lifting up their hands; and they bowed their heads, and worshiped the Lord with their faces to the ground." The people responded to the reading of the Word by worshiping the Lord. But verse 8 is the key: "So they read in the book in the law of God distinctly, and gave the sense, and caused them to understand the reading." Do you see what that says? That's why we must not only read the Word, we must also seek to know what it means by what it says.

In 1 Timothy 4:13 Paul told Timothy how to preach. He said, "Till I come, give attendance to reading, to exhortation, to doctrine." Do you see what he meant? He told Timothy to read the text, explain the text (doctrine), and apply the text (exhortation). You just don't read it and apply it; you read it, then explain it, and then apply it. That's what "rightly dividing the word" (2 Tim. 2:15) is all about. Otherwise, misinterpretation is the likely result, and misinterpretation is the mother of all kinds of mania. For example, let me give you some things that are being taught today based on misinterpretation. First, some people are teaching that since the patriarchs practiced polygamy, so must we. Or, since the Old Testament sanctioned the divine right to the king of Israel, all kings have divine rights. Or, since the Old Testament sanctioned the death of witches, we should be killing witches. Or, because some Old Testament plagues were from God, we should avoid sanitation so we don't thwart Him. How about this one: the Old Testament teaches that women would suffer in childbirth as a divine punishment, therefore, no anesthetic should ever be used. Now these are all misinterpretations because somebody doesn't understand what the Bible is really saying, and they don't understand the situation in which it was written.

Now it isn't necessarily easy to understand all of the Bible, and I remember one man, a Bible teacher, who said to me, "I'm so sick of trying to understand the Bible that I've decided to take everything for everybody. I've tried the dispensational route, I've tried the modified dispensational route, and I've tried the covenant theology route. So I've just decided to apply everything to everybody." I said, "Oh, when did you sacrifice your last lamb? Do you go through ceremonial washings of all the pots in your kitchen before your wife prepares your kosher meal?" You can't apply everything to everybody! There must be the proper interpretation.

But how do I get the proper interpretation? Let me show you three areas you need to understand. First, you must realize that there are:

A. Errors of Interpretation

To accurately interpret the Word, there are three errors to be avoided:

1. Don't make a point at the price of proper interpretation

In other words, don't make the Bible say what you want it to say. That's like the preacher who preached on the fact that women shouldn't have hair on top of their head. His text was "Top Knot Come Down" from Matthew 24:17 where it says, "Let him who is on the housetop not come down." That's not what that passage is teaching! That's ridiculous! Or, you can approach the Bible like the guy who said, "I've already got a sermon; I just have to find a verse for it." That's having a preconceived idea and then getting some verses to support it. I know if I try to *make* a sermon, I wind up forcing the Bible to fit my sermon. But if I try to comprehend a passage, out of the understanding of that passage flows a message. You can think of some great stuff and some fabulous outlines, but then you have to twist the Bible to make it say what you want it to say. Let's look at a couple of examples:

a) The Tower of Babel

I remember reading in the Talmud that one time the rabbis decided they wanted to preach a message on the fact that the people should care for each other. They had a social problem because people weren't loving people. So they said the best illustration in the Bible to show that people should love people is the story of the Tower of Babel. The Talmud interprets it this way: The reason God scattered all those people, and the reason He confounded their language, was because they had put materials before people. They said that as the Tower of Babel was growing taller, it took a hod carrier many hours to carry the load of bricks to the top so the bricklayers could lay their bricks. If a man fell off the tower on the way down, nobody paid any attention because they didn't lose any bricks. But if a guy fell over on the way up, they were furious because they lost their bricks. So that's why God scattered the nations and confounded their language, because they were more concerned about bricks than people. Well, that's true, you ought to be more concerned about people than bricks, but that's not what the Tower of Babel teaches us. God did not scatter them because they were more concerned about bricks. He scattered them because they were building an idolatrous religious system.

b) Salvation lost

I've heard sermons from 2 Peter 2:20 on how you can lose your salvation. Invariably, they'll quote the verse: "For if, after they have escaped the pollutions of the world through the knowledge of the Lord and Savior, Jesus Christ, they are again entangled in it and overcome, the latter end is worse with them than the beginning." Then they'll say, "You see, you can escape the pollutions, you can have the knowledge of the Lord and Savior, and you can fall and become entangled, and your latter is worse than before you believed. You see, you can lose your salvation." However, the thing they forget about is the word "they." If you study the word "they" from the beginning of chapter 2, you'll find that it's talking about "wells without water," clouds without rain (v. 17), and "spots they are and blemishes" (v. 13). If you trace it back to 2:1 you'll see that it's talking about false prophets who follow the doctrines of demons. You cannot use the verse to say that you can lose your salvation, because that is not its context. In fact, Paul has a word for those who do this. In 2 Corinthians 2:17*a* he says, "For we are not as many, who corrupt the word of God." The Greek word for corrupt is *kapēlos,* which basically had to do with selling something in the marketplace deceitfully; selling a product that really wasn't what it was claimed to be, or falsifying. Paul said that there are some who falsify the Word of God; they corrupt it to fit their own thoughts.

You must not make the Bible illustrate your sermon or your thoughts. Be careful not to interpret the Bible at the price of its true meaning—let it say what it means to say.

2. Avoid superficial interpretation

As you study the Bible to learn what it says, don't be superficial. Some people will say, "Well, I think this verse means—" or, "What does this verse mean to you?" Unfortunately, a lot of Bible studies are nothing but a pooling of ignorance; a lot of people sitting around telling what they don't know about the verse. Now I'm for Bible studies, but somebody has to study to find out what it really means, then you can discuss the application. First Timothy 5:17 even tells us about elders who work hard at the Word of God. So it's important not to be superficial.

The first error we mentioned was: Don't make a point at the price of the right interpretation. Second, avoid superficial interpretation. And last:

3. Don't spiritualize

The first sermon I ever preached was a horrible sermon. My text was "And the angel rolled the stone away." My sermon was "Rolling Away Stones in Your Life." I talked about the stone of doubt, the stone of fear, and the stone of anger. That is not what that verse is talking about; it's talking about a real stone. I made it a terrific allegory. Once I heard a sermon on "they cast four anchors . . . and wished for the day" (Acts 27:29); the anchor of hope, the anchor of faith, and so on. Those were not anchors of anything but metal. I call that "Little Bo Peep" preaching because you don't need the Bible, you can use anything. You can even use Little Bo Peep.

Let me show you what I mean. Someone can get up and say, "Little Bo Peep has lost her sheep." All over the world people are lost. (You see, you don't need the Bible.) "And can't tell where to find them. And they'll come home—" Ah, they'll come home. Then you tell a tear-jerking story about some sinners who came home "wagging their tails behind them." Do you see what I mean? It's so easy to do, and a lot of people do that with the Old Testament. They turn it into a fairy book and make all kinds of crazy things happen. Don't spiritualize the Bible; get the right meaning.

So there are three errors to avoid: Don't make a point at the price of a proper interpretation, avoid a superficial interpretation, and don't spiritualize.

Now to properly interpret the Bible, we'll have to bridge some gaps. To do that, we'll have to examine the:

B. Sources of Interpretation

The Bible has been around for many years, parts of it for as long as four thousand years. Now how are we going to understand what they were saying and the various circumstances in which they lived? Well, we have to bridge four gaps. First, we have to understand:

1. The language

We speak English, but the Bible was written in Hebrew and Greek, and a few parts in Aramaic (which is similar to Hebrew). So we have a language gap that must be bridged, otherwise, we won't fully be able to understand the Scripture. For example, in 1 Corinthians 4:1 the apostle Paul says, "Let a man so account of us, as of the ministers of Christ." Now that sounds great, Paul; you're a minister of Christ. When we think of the English word *minister,* we think of a prime minister or the minister of defense. A minister is an elevated thing; it's a dignified term. But the Greek word is *hupēretēs,* which means a third-level galley slave on a ship. Paul said that when the record goes in for him, let it be said that he was nothing more than a third-level galley slave for Jesus Christ. You would never get that out of the English term. Why? Because there's a language gap.

Another example is in the book of Hebrews. When you look at the word *perfection* in the book (6:1; 7:11), you can get completely confused on how you comprehend Hebrews unless you understand that perfection has to do with salvation, not spiritual maturity. That's what you'll find out as you study the words and their relationships in the text. It is very important to do this. And to study the words in the Bible, particularly in the New Testament, you should get W. E. Vine's *An Expository Dictionary of New Testament Words* (Moody Press, 1985). It's very helpful for someone who doesn't know Greek. You can look up every English word, and it will tell you the Greek meaning. It will be a great help to you as a Bible student. Also, a good concordance will help you in the study of words.

2. The culture

The cultural gap must be bridged, because cultures can be very different. If we don't understand the culture of the time in which the Bible was written, we'll never understand its meaning. For example: "In the beginning was the Word, and the Word was with God, and the Word was God" (John 1:1). What does that mean? Why didn't he say, "In the beginning was Jesus"? Well, he used "the Word" because that was the vernacular at that time. To the Greeks the term *Word* was used to refer to a floating kind of cause, a kind of ethereal, spatial kind of energy that was floating around. John said to the Greeks that that floating cause, that thing which caused everything, that spatial energy, that cosmic power, is none other than that Word which became flesh (1:14).

To the Jew, the term *Word* was always the manifestation of God, because "the Word of the Lord" was always God emanating His personality. So when John said "the Word was made flesh and dwelt among us," he was identifying Jesus Christ, the incarnate Christ, as the very emanation of God. In the text, therefore, he meets the Greek mind and Hebrew mind with the right word that grabs both at vital points. And this goes on all through the Bible. If you don't understand the Gnosticism existent at the time of the writing of Colossians, you won't understand the book. If you don't understand the culture at the time the Judaizers were moving into the Gentile churches, you can't understand the book of Galatians. If you don't understand the Jewish culture, you can't understand the book of Matthew. There must be cultural comprehension to fully understand the Bible.

Some books that would help you in this area are *The Life and Times of Jesus the Messiah* by Alfred Edersheim (Eerdmans, 1974) and *Barclay's Daily Study Bible Series* by William B. Barclay (Westminster, 1975). Barclay's insights into culture are very good even though his theology is askew in some areas.

3. The geography

There are geography gaps that must also be bridged. When we read in the Bible that they went down to Jericho, what does it mean to go *down* to Jericho? Well, when you go into Jericho you go *down*. When it says that they went *up* to Jerusalem it is because Jerusalem is definitely up. It's on a high plateau. In 1 Thessalonians 1:8 it says, "For from you sounded out the word of the Lord not only in Macedonia and Achaia, but also in every place your faith toward God is spread abroad." What's amazing is that it was sounded out so fast. Paul had just been there, and when he wrote the letter, very little time had passed. Paul had been with them for a couple of weeks, but their testimony had already spread far. How could that happen so fast? If you study the geography of the area you'll find that the Ignatian Highway runs right through the middle of Thessalonica. It was the main concourse between the East and West, and whatever happened there was passed all the way down the line. Do you see how a little bit of understanding of the geography enriches the comprehension?

Language, culture, geography, and one more:

4. The history

When you know the history behind a passage it will also help your comprehension. In the gospel of John, the whole key to understanding the interplay between Pilate and Jesus is based on the knowledge of history. When Pilate came into the land with his emperor worship, it literally infuriated the Jews and their priests. So he was off to a bad start from the very beginning. Then he tried to pull something on the Jews, and when they caught him, they reported him to Rome, and he almost lost his job. Pilate was afraid of the Jews, and that's why he let Christ be crucified. Why was he afraid? Because he already had a rotten track record, and his job was on the line.

Now that's the kind of history we need to understand to open the meaning of the Bible. And you can get this type of information from various sources. One is *The Zondervan Pictorial Encyclopedia of the Bible* (Zondervan, 1976). Or, a good Bible dictionary will help.

To interpret the Bible means closing the gaps. As you interpret the meaning of Scripture by using the various sources, you will close the language gap, the culture gap, the geography gap, and the history gap. But what are the principles you use?

C. Principles of Interpretation

   1. The literal principle

   First, you should use the literal principles. That means you
   should understand Scripture in its literal, normal, natural
   sense. Now there will be figures of speech, but that's normal
   language. There will be symbols, but that's normal language
   too. When you study apocalyptic passages like Zechariah,
   Daniel, Ezekiel, Isaiah, and Revelation, you will read about
   beasts and images. Now those are figures of speech and symbols, but they convey *literal* truth. Interpret the Bible in its
   normal, natural sense. Otherwise, you're taking an unnatural,
   abnormal, nonsensical interpretation. For example, the rabbis
   said that if you take the consonants of Abraham's name, b-r-
   h-m, and add them up, you get 318. Therefore, when you see
   the word Abraham, it means that he had 318 servants. That's
   not what it means. It means Abraham.

   So we must take the literal, normal, natural interpretation.
   We have to be careful when somebody comes along and says
   there's a secret meaning—and they use the verse "For the letter killeth, but the Spirit giveth life" (2 Cor. 3:6b). They use
   an allegorical method to get the hidden, secretive meaning. Do
   you know what that is? Nobody knows! They make it up.
   Don't do that—interpret Scripture in its literal sense.

   2. The historical principle

   The Bible must be studied in its historical context. What did it
   mean to the people to whom it was spoken or written? It is
   said that a text without a context (historically) is a pretext.
   You have to understand the historical setting in many cases,
   or you'll never really understand what's in the writer's heart.

   3. The grammatical principle

   To study the grammar we must look at the sentence, the
   prepositions, pronouns, verbs, and nouns. In school we had
   to learn how to diagram a sentence so we could find out what
   it was saying. For example, in Matthew 28:19-20 we have the
   great commission: "Go therefore and make disciples of all the
   nations, baptizing them . . . teaching them to observe all that
   I commanded you" (NASB). As you first read it, "Go"
   sounds like a verb; "make disciples, baptizing, teaching," all
   sound like verbs. But as you study the sentence, you find
   there's only one verb, *mathēteusate,* "make disciples." "Go"
   is nothing more than a participle, "baptizing" is a participle,
   and "teaching" is a participle, which means they modify the

73

main verb. What the great commission says is "make disciples," and in making disciples you will have to go, baptize, and teach. When you understand that, the fullness of that concept comes out of the text.

Another illustration I can give you is in Matthew 18:20. How many times have you heard somebody say this in a prayer meeting: " 'Where two or three are gathered together in my name, there am I in the midst of them.' Friends, two or three of us are here, so the Lord is here"? Do you want to know something? If I'm there *alone,* the Lord is there! That verse has nothing to do with a prayer meeting. If you study the context and the grammar you find that out. What it's saying is that when you discipline somebody, when you put somebody out of the church, and his sin has been confirmed by two or three witnesses, Christ said that He is in the midst. You'll learn that if you study the text. So you have to examine the grammar carefully to fully comprehend the meaning of the text.

4. The synthesis principle

The synthesis principle is what the Reformists called the *Analogia Scriptura*—the Scripture all comes together. In other words, one part of the Bible doesn't teach something that another part contradicts. So as you study the Scripture it must all fit together. For example, when you're reading through 1 Corinthians and you come to 15:29, where Paul talks about the baptism for the dead, do you say, "Well, there's a new doctrine. You can get baptized for a dead person and that will save him"? Now wait a minute. Does the Bible allow for somebody to be baptized for a dead person? Where is that in Scripture? Doesn't that contradict the doctrine of salvation? That can't be the interpretation of that passage because no passage, in and of itself, will contradict the teaching of Scripture. That's the synthesis principle.

J. I. Packer has wonderfully said, "The Bible appears like a symphony orchestra, with the Holy Ghost as its Toscanini, each instrument has been brought willingly, spontaneously, creatively, to play his notes just as the great conductor desired, though none of them could ever hear the music as a whole. . . . The point of each part only becomes fully clear when seen in relation to all the rest" (from *God Has Spoken*).

Do you know what that tells me? There are *no* contradictions. What appear as contradictions can be resolved if we have the information, because the Bible comes together as a whole.

5. The practical principle

Are you saying, "This is all so foggy, the literal principle and all these other things. When does it ever get down to where I'm living?" Well, this is the practical principle. The final question is: So what? As you try to interpret the Bible, how do you find out what it means for your life? Make sure in your Bible study that you find the practical principle. I have a little phrase that I use: "Learn to principlize the Scripture." Read it and find out what spiritual principle is there that applies to you. But you can't do that until you've gone through the other principles first: literal, historical, grammatical, and synthesis. You know what it means by what it says—now you come to how it applies to you.

Now that's how you interpret the Bible. While you're reading through the Bible, now and then work on some of the problem passages. Read a little in a Bible dictionary, or a commentary, and begin to put some things together. What is the literal meaning? What is the historical setting? What is the grammatical structure? How does it fit in with the rest of Scripture? and, How does it apply to me?

So, read the Bible, interpret the Bible, and third:

III. Meditate on the Bible

Don't be in a hurry when you study God's Word. Deuteronomy 6:6-7 says, "And these words, which I command thee this day, shall be in thine heart; and thou shalt teach them diligently unto thy children, and shalt talk of them when thou sittest in thine house, and when thou walkest by the way, and when thou liest down, and when thou risest up." In other words, you ought to have God's Word running around in your mind all the time. Do you want to know a secret? If you're reading through the Old Testament, and if you're reading a book of the New Testament through thirty times in a row, all the time, then you're going to have it running around in your mind. Meditation is what takes all of those parts and begins to mold them together into a cohesive comprehension of biblical truth. God also says in Deuteronomy 6:8-9, "And thou shalt bind them for a sign upon thine hand, and they shall be as frontlets between thine eyes. And thou shalt write them upon the posts of thy house, and on thy gates." God says He wants His Word everywhere. But we live in a culture where we drive down the street, and our eyes are literally assaulted with garbage—whiskey ads, beer ads, girlie shows, rotten movies—and the garbage just pours into our heads. God said that we should take His Word and let it be a billboard in front of our eyes, let it be filling our mind, our voice, wherever we go. That's the way it ought to be.

A man was asked one time, "When you can't sleep, do you count sheep?" He said, "No. I talk to the Shepherd." That's what God wants His people to do, talk to the Shepherd—meditate. Psalm 1:1-2 says, "Blessed is the man who walketh not in the counsel of the ungodly, nor standeth in the way of sinners, nor sitteth in the seat of the scornful. But his delight is in the law of the Lord; and in his law doth he meditate day and night." Like the cow chewing its cud, just going over it and over it and over it, so too should we meditate on the Word, going over it and over it and over it.

So, we are to read the Bible, interpret the Bible, meditate on the Bible, and last, we are to:

IV. Teach the Bible

Do you know what I discovered? The best way to learn it is to give it away. I've found that the things that I learn well enough to teach are the things I retain. But do you know that it's very easy to not be understood? If you hear somebody speak and you don't understand anything he says, then *he* probably doesn't understand his subject. But it's hard to be clear, because to be clear you have to master your subject. So, as a teacher, you are forced to master your subject. Then if you teach, you'll retain it. Just feed somebody else and see how it feeds your own heart. I believe that personal motivation for study comes from responsibility. If I didn't have somebody to teach, I wouldn't produce.

Well, I hope this helps to get you started in studying God's Word. Read the Bible, interpret the Bible, meditate on the Bible, and teach the Bible. But when you think you've done it all, don't get a big head and say, "Well, I've arrived. I've mastered it all." Just remember Deuteronomy 29:29a: "The secret things belong unto the Lord our God." When you've said it all, and done it all, and learned it all, you haven't scratched the surface of the infinite mind of God. But do you know what the purpose is? Your purpose in learning the Word of God is not to have knowledge for the sake of knowledge, because Paul said, "Knowledge puffeth up" (1 Cor. 8:1a). Your purpose is to *know* God, and to know God is to learn humility.

Focusing on the Facts

1. What does Bible study begin with (see p. 62)?

2. Describe a good method for reading through the Old Testament (see pp. 62-63).

3. What is the "mystery" that Paul referred to in Colossians 1:26? What was the major thrust of his ministry (see p. 63)?

4. Why is it important to spend more time when reading the New Testament as compared to the Old Testament (see p. 63)?

5. Describe a good method for reading a book in the New Testament (see pp. 63-64).

6. What is a good way to learn anything, particularly the Bible (see p. 64)?

7. Why is it good to continue reading from the same version of the Bible (see p. 65)?

8. What will happen when you begin to read the Bible repetitiously (see p. 65)?

9. What question does Bible interpretation answer (see p. 66)?

10. What did the people of Israel do in Nehemiah 8:8 (see p. 66)?

11. What did Paul command Timothy to do in 1 Timothy 4:13? What did he mean (see p. 66)?

12. How did the Talmud misinterpret the story of the Tower of Babel? What is the correct interpretation (see p. 68)?

13. How do some people misinterpret 2 Peter 2:20? What is the correct interpretation (see pp. 68-69)?

14. What does Paul say about those who try to make the Bible fit their way of thinking (2 Cor. 2:17; see p. 69)?

15. Why is it important to avoid superficial interpretations (see p. 69)?

16. Give an example of spiritualizing a passage of Scripture (see pp. 69-70).

17. Give some examples that illustrate the language gap we face when we study the Bible (see pp. 70-71).

18. What is one good way of bridging the language gap (see pp. 70-71)?

19. How does John 1:1 illustrate the cultural gap that exists between our day and the first century (see p. 71)?

20. Give an illustration of how an understanding of the geography of the day is important to our interpretation of the Bible (see p. 72).

21. What gap needs to be closed to understand the interplay between Pilate and Jesus (see p. 72)?

22. What is the first principle that should be used in interpreting the Bible? Explain (see p. 73).

23. Why is it important to know the historical context of a passage of Scripture (see p. 73)?

24. Explain Matthew 28:19-20 in terms of its grammar (see pp. 73-74).

25. Explain the synthesis principle of Bible interpretation (see p. 74).

26. As you interpret the Bible, how do you find out what it means for your life (see p. 75)?

27. According to Deuteronomy 6:8-9, where does God want His Word (see p. 75)?

28. What is the best way to learn what the Bible says (see p. 76)?

Pondering the Principles

1. Make up a plan for reading both the Old and New Testament. Decide what time or times of the day you want to put aside for reading. Start in Genesis for your reading in the Old Testament. Pick any book in the New Testament for your daily reading. Just be sure to break it down if necessary so you can read for thirty minutes each day for thirty days. Begin your reading schedule today.

2. If you have been wanting to study a particular portion of Scripture but didn't know how, now you can. Plan the time that you want to spend on your study. If you don't have some of the study tools mentioned on pages 71-72, you may want to visit a library. In your study, be sure to avoid the errors of interpretation. As you study, work at bridging the linguistic, cultural, geographical, and historical gaps. Finally, use the proper principles of interpretation as you study. Remember, the goal of your study is not only to learn what the Bible means, but also to learn what it means to you.

Scripture Index

Moody Press, a ministry of the Moody Bible Institute, is designed for education, evangelization, and edification. If we may assist you in knowing more about Christ and the Christian life, please write us without obligation: Moody Press, c/o MLM, Chicago, Illinois 60610.